HOW TO
SAVE ON
YOUR HOME

THE DREYFUS FAMILY MONEY MANAGEMENT SERVICE

HOW TO SAVE ON THE HOME YOU WANT

By DARRELL HUFF
with Frances Huff

and the Editors of Dreyfus Publications

illustrated by Roy Doty

DREYFUS PUBLICATIONS LTD.   NEW YORK

DARRELL HUFF gained his expertise on housing through experience and practice. He has lived in various kinds of dwellings, is the author of *Complete Book of Home Improvements* (Harper & Row) and has so far built three homes for himself—and then sold them profitably. A veteran free-lance writer, he has written for many magazines. His books include *How to Lie with Statistics* (Norton), *How to Take a Chance* (Norton) and *How to Figure the Odds on Everything,* the last-named for the Dreyfus Family Money Management Service. His wife Frances collaborated with him on the present volume, as she has on other projects.

THE DREYFUS FAMILY MONEY MANAGEMENT SERVICE

Jay Gold
EDITORIAL DIRECTOR

Sandylee Williams
EDITORIAL ASSISTANT

Spero Yianilos
ASSISTANT EDITOR

John M. Hix
ART CONSULTANT

DREYFUS PUBLICATIONS LTD.

Jerome S. Hardy
PRESIDENT

George Erikson
LEGAL DEPARTMENT

Heinz Eller
EXECUTIVE VICE-PRESIDENT

Robert F. Dubuss
Julian Smerling
FINANCIAL DEPARTMENT

Sally J. Reich
Martin Stone
VICE-PRESIDENTS

Arlene Armstrong
BUSINESS OFFICE

CONTENTS

A NOTE TO THE READER

This book, like its companion volumes in this series, has been planned to be as functional as it is informative. For that reason, the typographic design for the text specifies exceptionally wide margins. These are meant to be used for anything that will be helpful to you: for notetaking, reminders to yourself or even doing arithmetical calculations. The editors hope you will find the margins useful.

The stock for these books was selected in part because it can be written on equally well with pencil, or ballpoint or felt-tipped pen.

The colored rules you will find scattered throughout the book are used to emphasize salient portions of the text.

—— THE EDITORS

CHAPTER 1

Rent? Own? Or Something Between?

Apartment or single-family dwelling?

Rent or buy?

These are the twin decisions almost every family makes at intervals—intervals that become smaller and smaller as our society becomes more and more mobile.

Fairly new—and interesting—is the fact that these two decisions can now be made independently of each other. Not only can you buy or rent if you choose to live in a house, but today you can own your own home even if you choose to live in an apartment.

So you can begin by deciding between apartment and separate house, leaving the question of whether it will be better for you to rent or to own to be considered later.

If you've already decided one way ("I hate apartments") or the other ("A house is too much trouble") today may be a splendid time to re-open your mind.

A little looking at the best of today's dwellings will bring you surprises. Modern materials and canny landscaping make some modern houses at least as easy to care for and as safe to leave for intervals of travel as a typical apartment. On the other hand, well-designed apartments now make such use of outdoor living space and noise barriers as to yield more privacy than many free-standing houses do.

But these are exceptions, of course. In any case, considering the checklist that follows will help you decide whether you are by nature an apartment-dweller or a houseowner at your present stage of life. If any numbered statement describes you as a family, credit apartment-living with one point. If the opposite is nearer the truth, credit house-living with one point. Where you feel yourself middle-of-the-road or uninterested, credit neither side.

Comparing the totals won't lead you magically to the wisest decision. But it may help you clarify your thinking by reminding you of some of the facts of housing.

1. You plan to—perhaps must—move more frequently than most people.

2. You feel happier with a minimum of possessions.

3. You have travel plans.

4. You are tolerant of noise from neighbors.

5. You're pretty quiet people.

Use the checklists to find the housing preference
of you and your spouse. What to do
if you disagree strongly
is a problem beyond the scope of this book.

6. Specifically, you don't produce loud music.

7. You don't own or want any pets not acceptable in an apartment building.

8. You have no interest in gardening that cannot be done in pots and boxes.

9. You have no avid interest in woodworking or other hobbies requiring a good deal of space.

10. You have no children at home or pending.

11. You don't often have young guests staying in your home.

12. You don't care for home-maintenance chores.

13. A convenient and close-in location is useful to you.

14. You are not interested in building or remodeling.

15. Your outside interests are so pressing that you spend limited time at home.

16. You don't know what you'll be doing—or where—a year from now.

17. Minimal housekeeping is more important to you than generous living space.

18. You don't feel a loss of individuality in occupying a unit similar to that of other families.

19. You don't own a lot of valuable furniture or other belongings requiring extensive storage space.

20. You don't have special tastes or standards that virtually require that your dwelling must be designed just for you.

If most of your replies are "yes," it suggests that apartment living may fit your current needs more closely than you might have thought. With predominantly "no" responses you should be quite hesitant about moving into an apartment—or quick to leave one.

A mid-scale rating is equally suggestive. It goes with no strong convictions on the subject—or with an optimistic yearning for the best of both worlds.

A house like an apartment

My own score, for example, shows a moderate leaning toward a separate house. My wife's is just about equally tilted the other way. Fortunately, the home we're just starting to build is a house in the form of a large studio apartment on a very small lot involving no upkeep at all. It is to be, in fact, a dwelling calculated to meet precisely the needs and wishes and lifestyle my informal little quiz reveals. Otherwise I'd be reconsidering some details or even the whole project.

Once you've decided whether your new home should be house or apartment you can turn to the other major question: rent or buy. If neither sounds right to you, take heart. There are a couple of other possibilities that blend features of both and are rapidly growing in popularity to fit in with today's way of living. We'll get to them in the next chapters.

The rent or buy question will have less influence on your way of living, possibly, but its economic effects may be more important in the long run. It's not always an easy decision. Consider the Bob Husers and their Uncle Jim.

Twenty-three years ago Jim and his wife, newly married, concluded that renters have it best. Since then he has continued in the same job, they have

moved only twice in all those years (one landlord decided to sell; the other was too incredibly stingy with paint). Since they've changed neither area nor kind of house, Jim and his wife are living today in essentially the same house in which they started their married life.

By paper and pencil to a startling conclusion

After an evening of talk with Uncle Jim, followed by some paper-and-pencil figuring, Bob Huser arrived at a startling conclusion. Before stating that conclusion, let's see how Bob reached it.

At the time, 23 years earlier, when Uncle Jim and his wife moved into their house, they could have bought it or something like it for $18,000. Using his veteran's privileges under the GI Bill, Jim would have had no down payment to make and closing costs would have been minor.

Even at 6% for 20 years—and the rate in those years was generally well under that—Jim's monthly payments would have been $129.06. Taxes and insurance would have added about $35 a month in the early years, possibly $55 by the end (as both rates and the value of the house increased), for an average of $45 a month over the 20 years of the mortgage.

By straining his memory of what his landlord must have laid out, Jim had arrived at a reasonable estimate of maintenance costs for such a house for 20 years. At $250 a year—for frequent small repairs plus an occasional major one such as exterior painting or a new roof—these came to an average of about $21 a month.

Adding these figures of Jim's together, his nephew Bob arrived at a monthly cost-to-own of something less than $185 for the early years, rising to $205 or so by the twentieth year. Average: $195.

But Jim had chosen to rent instead. His landlord, hewing fairly closely to the old rule of thumb that gross monthly rentals should approximate 1% of value, had charged him $175 a month when he moved in. As property values (and taxes and maintenance) increased over the years, so did the rent Jim paid for his initial rented house and its successors. The $275 Jim currently pays actually represents well under 1% of the market value of the house he's in, although it is similar to the one he might have bought years ago for $18,000.

He could have owned it for nothing

Since Jim's rent increases have been gradual but consistent, following the pattern in most localities, his average rent has been about $225.

And that is how Bob Huser arrived at a startling conclusion: Uncle Jim could have owned the house he's now living in and it wouldn't have cost him a cent more. Furthermore, there would be no more rent to pay in the future.

It's an inescapable conclusion, and it would be true for almost anyone in Uncle Jim's position who had made the same decision and stayed with it.

A dazzling difference

He had, as the saying goes, nothing to show for all those years of rent checks except a bundle of receipts. The same checks would have bought the house, with some dollars to spare for added maintenance costs (if they had in fact proved heavier than the estimate) and even an extensive remodeling. The difference between Jim's actual rental outlay ($225 a month) and his estimated payments if he had bought ($195) comes to a dazzling $7,200.

On top of that, Uncle Jim could have—depending upon the size of his income and the nature of his expenditures for doctor bills and contributions and other deductible items—gained by lowering his state and federal income-tax payment. Bob Huser had only to multiply Jim's $129.06 a month by the 240 months the mortgage ran to discover that the total outlay for principal and interest had been $30,974. Taking away the $18,000 that was repayment of principal, $12,794 must have gone for interest. All of this might have been tax deductible. The net saving would depend, of course, on Uncle Jim's tax bracket.

"Gosh," concluded Bob Huser. "Uncle Jim has thrown away a house." His wife Beatrice saw it the

And after all those years of regular payments
for rent, he had nothing to show
but a pile of receipts.

same way, and the young couple proceeded to buy an attractive new house of their own.

Then three things happened

Within the next twelve months three things happened. Costs of houses over the United States as a whole went up 8%. A large government project having to do with space flight was discontinued along the seashore 10 miles from where the Husers lived. And Bob and Beatrice decided to move to Wyoming where Bob had found a teaching job equal to the one he had been holding and where he could do the outdoor work he loved as a park ranger each summer.

The Husers promptly put their house up for sale, only to discover that because of the local drop in employment three other families within the small subdivision had just done the same thing—at prices reflecting eagerness to sell.

Persistence, time, money, inconvenience

Only by persistence, plus some time and money on repairs and fix-up, and at considerable personal inconvenience, did Bob and Beatrice sell their house at a fair price. Happily for them, the general rise in building costs almost canceled out the effects of the weakness in the local house market.

The price their house fetched equaled the cost of building it a year earlier . . . or what they had paid for it less about what the seller had added to his net

price to cover the real-estate salesman's 6% commission.

When a selling commission is skimmed off the
top of a sale price, it is elementary economics
that buyer or seller, or the two jointly, must absorb a loss of that amount. This will often be
reflected in a somewhat higher price when the
seller, or the two jointly, must absorb the loss
and will often be reflected in a somewhat
higher price than the seller would accept if he
were dealing on his own. It is, in effect, the difference between a retail price and a wholesale
one.

Since the price the Husers paid had been, as a result of all this, some 6% more than the seller's calculation of the value of the house to him, the Husers
started out that much in the hole. This 6% handicap,
along with a similar commission that the Husers paid
for their virtually forced resale, put them essentially
in the position of having bought at retail and sold at
wholesale. This produced a loss to them of about
12% of the value of the house. This plus some closing
costs that are a part of most house sales came to just
over $3,000 on their average-priced (about $24,000)
home. The down payment on the house came to just
about that, so you could call this the Case of the
Vanished Down Payment.

"Well," said Bob philosophically, "let's just think of it as a year's rent. Is $250 a month so bad?"

It is, actually, when you add the year's taxes and insurance payment ($740) and mortgage interest, plus interest lost on the amount of the down payment. And money and time invested in all the improvements buyers normally make in a new and unlandscaped house that an older rental dwelling would not require. Even after balancing against this some $400 saved by being able to deduct $2,300 interest and property taxes from their taxable income, the Husers put out upwards of $450 a month for a house they might have rented for under $200.

As investment mistakes go, this one was not a first-class disaster—as it might have been if Bob's choice of house and value-for-price had not been as good as it was. But at best it's no argument for home-ownership.

What the Husers' story does offer is a summing up of the best single general rule for deciding whether buying or renting is the wiser course for you:

If you're confident of staying fixed for at least several years, buy. If you're indecisive, and your job is not all that permanent, rent.

But keep in mind some possible exceptions: With interest rates on the climb, lean toward buying. If you'll have to take a second mortgage (more about

If you're good at fixing up, you can
make yourself money by finding a sick house
that you can restore to good health.

this in a later chapter) at an interest rate well above
that prevailing for first mortgages, consider renting
while you save enough for an adequate down payment.

If you're a fixer-upper you may be able to buy a
house and turn a nice profit on it in a year or two.
Many families have done so repeatedly, although it's
not an activity everybody enjoys. Furthermore, full-
scale remodeling is beyond the scope of all but the
professionals.

If you can buy and sell without paying commissions, the odds favor your coming out ahead by buying. But you should first learn quite a bit about houses and their financing and selling. You can't hope to cut out the real-estate agent profitably without yourself learning some of the things he knows and without putting out some of the efforts he makes to earn his living.

Your two decisions, then, will probably add up to one of these four combinations: rent a house; rent an apartment; buy a house; buy an apartment.

If you lean toward the first or second of these combinations, you'll find your immediate interests covered primarily in the chapter on renting strategy and (since assessing the livability of a house is almost as important to a potential renter as to a possible buyer) the one on how to look at a house, with its accompanying checklists in the appendix. Material in other chapters will be useful to you in testing your decision with the idea possibly of changing it now or later . . . as you or circumstances or the composition of your family change. The last two chapters may bear directly on interests of yours, since second homes and vacation living are becoming more universal concerns.

The material on wise renting may seem irrelevant at the moment, if you've put all that behind you by choosing to be a homeowner. But consider: as owner of a house or an apartment that you may have occasion to vacate for a period, you can become deeply concerned with rental arrangements from a landlord's point of view. And you may become an occasional renter, too, if you take extended vacations in other parts of this country as well as other parts of the world, as many families plan to do.

With the best will in the world it is quite possible you just won't be able to come to a firm decision on the rent-or-buy question. One possible out for you is a lease-option.

Lease-option is a rental arrangement in which you pay a little extra for the privilege of converting yourself into a purchaser after a period. The chapter on rental strategy tells a little more about how to do this.

You could be a special case

Or you may be a householder for whom none of the conventional solutions is quite right. You may want to undertake something quite unfamiliar to most of us: ownership of a home—either freestanding or in apartment form—without ownership of land. The next two chapters go into how this is achieved and what it might do for you.

CHAPTER II

Co-ops and Condominiums: Buying an Apartment

It's a new and strange idea to most Americans—buying one apartment in an apartment building.

The suddenly familiar word for it, condominium, is simply a Latin compound meaning joint ownership and control.

Actually it's no new thing. In Europe as far back as the 12th century each floor of a house, and sometimes each room, could be owned by a different family or person. There is a Babylonian document from 2000 B.C. that mentions sale of the first floor of a house with the original owner retaining title to the second floor.

Condominium ownership is a blend of private and cooperative ownership. It is rapidly replacing pure cooperative ownership, in which you and some other people own an apartment house jointly and each of you has the right to lease an apartment, sharing tax and mortgage payments, upkeep, and so on.

Joining a cooperative is buying into a corporation. You are purchasing a share of a business that owns and operates the building in which you live. The larger your apartment the greater your share in the business.

A cooperative apartment house has officers. It is operated for a profit, which you share by getting greater benefits or by paying lower operating costs. In other words, you're your own landlord, along with all the other tenants who have bought into the apartment venture. So you're not really buying an apartment at all. You're buying shares in a business which owns and runs the building in which you live.

In addition to buying your shares, you will have to pay a monthly fee to cover your part of the property taxes and maintenance for the whole building.

Why buy into a co-op instead of renting an apartment? Because you will gain not only a place to live but also a vote on how the building shall be maintained, who will be permitted to buy into the venture (and thus become your neighbor), and how much of the profits shall be spent and on what.

As with a condominium, but not with a rented apartment, there's a tax break, too. You can deduct from your income for tax purposes the portion of your maintenance fee used to pay mortgage interest and taxes on the whole property. And if your building is well run and increases in value, your shares will be worth more.

The condominium idea that seemed "new" to the US in the late '60s has in fact a lineage going back at least as far as to ancient Babylon.

Are there disadvantages?

You can't buy or sell or do any drastic remodeling without the approval of the officers elected by you to run the project. Maintenance costs may go up. If your building becomes less desirable, because of location or the way in which it is run, value of your shares may drop.

Your neighbors and your investment

Much of the value of your own investment depends upon the financial responsibility of your neighbors. If they take bankruptcy, fail to pay their monthly maintenance fees, or generally contribute to the decrease in desirability of the apartment building, you will share with other tenants the problems—financial and physical—of being in a business that no longer attracts the right kind of people.

Some, but not all, of these problems can arise with a condominium as well.

The difference is that with a condominium you have full title to your own apartment. You pay the mortgage. You pay the taxes.

In addition you, jointly with your neighbors, own the land and all improvements that are not distinctly a part of your apartment. These improvements commonly include floors, roofs, main walls, elevators, lobbies, staircases, halls, parking spaces, garages, and all sorts of recreational facilities, from swimming pool to sauna bath.

You pay a monthly fee to cover cost of maintaining the land and common facilities.

A condominium offers a special blend of many of the advantages of apartment renting with those of owning a home—and inevitably some of their drawbacks as well.

If you have found—possibly with assistance from our little quiz in the previous chapter—that your tastes and circumstances incline toward ownership, you will want to investigate condominiums in your chosen area.

Here are some of the characteristics of condominiums—elements to consider as you look and decide:

1. Each apartment has its own mortgage. So you have no liability to worry about if your neighbor falls behind.

2. Same thing goes for property tax.

3. You can sell your apartment just as if it were a house. (But there is likely to be a stipulation that you must give the management first refusal when you sell.)

4. You have the privilege of selecting your neighbors. (But with this goes the chance you could become part—willingly or otherwise—of a conspiracy to keep out any kind of people most of your neighbors wished to exclude.)

5. Since you are buying for cash or on a mortgage at a fixed monthly figure, there is no rent to be increased. (But taxes can go up, just as with a single-

family dwelling. And maintenance fees can rise with costs or when a majority of your neighbors decides on a new swimming pool or more tennis courts.)

6. Condominiums usually offer comparatively solid walls and private entrances. But beware: some are no better than poor apartment houses, although marketed in this appealing new way. A condominium is only as good as the design ability and skill of its builder.

7. Since you own your condominium apartment you get the advantage of essentially the same income-tax deductions as any homeowner.

8. You also have the protection against inflation that other homeowners have by owning real estate likely to go up in worth.

9. Condominiums usually offer jointly owned facilities—pools, tennis courts, saunas, laundries, recreation rooms. But not always: most of these are pretty limited in low-priced condominiums because buyers can't afford the cost; and they are limited in high-priced ones because rich people have their clubs and recreation areas away from home.

10. Owning an apartment means you are not paying, as in a rental, for the cost of vacancies. These costs to landlords, passed on to renters, run about 5% nationally, 10% in some areas.

11. Since you have your own mortgage you can buy mortgage insurance to pay it off if you die.

12. Except in the rare cases when a condominium is a separate or row house* on jointly held land, it can

---

* A row house ordinarily stands on its own land and is separately owned, yet shares sidewalls with neighboring houses.

have all the physical drawbacks of any apartment. Check for privacy problems and noise penetration before you sign anything. If the condominium isn't built yet, check with the occupants and owners of condominiums or apartments previously built by the same contractor.

13. Condominiums are sometimes sold before they are started or while under construction, so if the builder fails to complete the project you could lose your down payment. So have a lawyer examine your contract. Try to have the down payment held by a bank or escrow company until the builder gets his certificate of occupancy. At least investigate carefully the builder's reputation.

Some condominium-dwellers are terrific at generating decibels.

14. You can freely dispose of your condominium by gift or will, just as you could if it were a house.

15. Condominiums have the same degree of protection against seizure for debt (in some states) and the same partial exemption from property taxes (in some others) that houses have.

16. Your share of cost of maintenance of yards, pools, and other elements held in common is fixed in the master deed. It is based on the relationship between the value of your apartment and that of the total of the apartments. This relationship cannot be changed except by consent of all.

17. But the amount of your monthly contribution toward upkeep and care of common facilities can go

up or down with changes in tax rates, maintenance costs, or number and kind of facilities offered.

18. There is no way out of paying this share of cost. Neither going away on vacation nor moving out will affect your obligation. Neither will waiving the right to use the common elements. So long as you own your unit your liability remains, just as does your liability to pay county or city property taxes on your apartment in a condominium.

19. Since you have your own separate deed, you can mortgage (and later refinance if you wish) just as with a house.

20. If you wish to sell, a new purchaser can get a new mortgage—perhaps for a much larger amount than you have paid yours down to. (In a cooperative apartment this is possible only in some states, so resale is often difficult except to a buyer who can pay mostly cash.)

Those are among the special considerations to keep in mind when contemplating any condominium purchase. The general physical aspects, the things that add up to convenience and comfort, are covered in the chapters on house buying; the legal and financial ones are in the material on those aspects of home ownership.

For many, purchase of a condominium is an alternative to becoming part-owner of a cooperative apartment. As indicated earlier, these two have a great deal in common.

One potential problem they share was brought out graphically not long ago by a communication from a

In a condominium you have to pay your own property taxes,
and your prorated share of maintenance in general
and for special facilities in particular.

middle-aged widow to the building magazine *House & Home.*

Since it is a story equally familiar to many dwellers in cooperative apartments, it is a valuable warning about the caution called for in choosing either a co-op or a condominium.

"A year ago, if anyone had asked how I like condominium living, I'd have unhesitatingly replied that there are no disadvantages. As a single person who once owned a ten-room house on an acre of land, it was a great relief for me not to have to cope with all the things that can go wrong with one's property, e.g., oak-worms, septic tank leaks, barking dogs.

"The condominium I chose is located in the middle of a golf course. Children under 12 are not allowed. . . . The majority of residents are older couples with a concern for keeping up the property and keeping the peace. . . .

"I assumed that the men, having been moderately successful in their various careers, could manage budgeting the $58,000 per year which the 60 owners kick into the maintenance fund at the rate of $80 a month. Their wives seemed relaxed and free of neurotic curiosity one finds among apartment-house busybodies.

Enter one nutty lady

"Then, a nutty lady moved in. The place has never been the same. I became aware of her when she distributed a 20-page letter advising owners that she had found a number of irregularities about the way the place was being managed. . . .

"About half of the owners had, at one time or another, served on the Board of Governors, and apparently had put in a great amount of time and energy developing a system. . . . The system was based on a sort of gentlemen's agreement that everyone involved was acting in good faith.

"But then the nutty lady's husband was asked to serve on the Board and his wife got hold of the books. Then she distributed her 20-page letter.

"Well, there was no way to avoid a confrontation, and that meeting was a shambles. Everyone had to take sides, and those who didn't, like me, were in real trouble. . . . It got to be funny, and I left before it was over because I couldn't stop laughing. Nothing was solved.

"The biggest disadvantage to condominium living is that apparently there is no productive way to handle dissent. Too much depends on leadership talent that happens to buy into the property. . . .

"One man who lives here really has good sense. . . .

"The solution, he says, is to find a professional property management company.

"So ends my commentary on condominium life. The financial advantages are great for people whose income bracket is high. They are not for people on a tight budget.

"At the rate this year's Board of Governors is spending our budget, we'll have to vote a fat increase next year to break even. And it's funny how financial problems can ruin social relationships. Living here is like being in a three-legged gunny sack race and discovering your large partner is a centipede."

The moral has two parts: Difficult neighbors become extraordinarily troublesome when you live very close to them; and managed housing is only as good as the quality and professionalism of its management.

CHAPTER III

The Immobile Mobile Home

What were 7,000,000 Americans living in by the early 1970s that were neither single-family houses on their own land, nor apartments, condominiums, or other multiple dwellings?

They're not houses built on leased land. That's an arrangement that otherwise meets the description, but it's still so rare as to call for only passing mention here. You can expect to hear a great deal more about this in the future in consequence of the growing shortage of prime residential land.

As a concept, the house on leased land is perhaps more attractive to the landowner than to the house buyer, at least as long as we continue to live in a period of general inflation coupled with growing land values. Reason: he keeps ownership of the land—the part that is growing in value; you own the building— the part that may depreciate in value through obsolescence and use.

The new kind of home ownership that has captured 7,000,000 of your fellow-citizens is the mobile home.

What, precisely, is a mobile home?

The *real* mobile home dweller is the snail,
who is always on the move with his home. Most mobile homes
move only once, to their permanent site.

It's *not* a trailer. People who live in mobile homes, and especially people who operate mobile home parks, will hate you if you confuse the two.

A mobile home arrives on wheels and it stays on wheels or jacks or concrete blocks or some other temporary support even though it is intended to be moved only occasionally if ever. And it is usually hooked up to all utilities and is used for year-round living.

And it's not a modular house. A modular may arrive on wheels but it is then slipped onto a permanent foundation. One reason for confusion is that both modulars and mobiles are relatively new and growing ways of reducing house building costs; and both are made in factories—often the same factory.

Modular, or factory, houses have a chapter of their own.

To plunge right in, the salient facts about mobiles are these.

For retirees only?

Mobiles are not just, or even primarily, for people of retirement age. (Only about 10% of the people who live in mobiles are over 65, though the percentage of older people in mobile-home *parks* is quite a bit larger.)

About half of all mobile homes stand on separate country or small-town lots. Only a little under half wind up in mobile-home parks. The rest are in a new—and now growing—kind of environment: the mobile-home subdivision.

Teenagers in mobiles

Just over half (53%) of mobile-home families include one or more children under 18.

Mobile homes cost only about half as much as other new houses of about the same size.

All the same, the owner of a conventional home spending the same total per month for housing may actually come out well ahead of the buyer of a mobile. But not all buyers of mobile homes are thinking primarily of costs and taxes and depreciation. Some say that what they are buying is a whole way of life. Since you might want—now or later—to join this growing way of life, let's see what it is and where and what it costs—both in the beginning and in the long run.

If, like half of this year's half-million buyers, you have your unit placed in a mobile-home park or subdivision, you will probably find a great degree of uniformity among your neighbors. In family structure, in age, in income, and even in how they think

and how they vote, they are likely to resemble each other.

This will probably be true to a far greater degree than in a neighborhood of conventional homes.

Is this bad? Not necessarily. If you can find a mobile park in which the majority of residents are your kind of people, you may find this homogeneity a positive advantage.

As a young couple you may prefer to have plenty of other young couples much like yourselves close by. As a retired couple you may

The population mix in a mobile home park
is usually not a mix: like tends to find like.

like to be surrounded by others who have
ample leisure to share with you. If you have
young or school-age children you will almost
certainly prefer to live where they will have
contemporaries close at hand.

On the other hand, if you don't care for uniformity
in a community you should take pains to investigate
the park you're considering for this characteristic
before you commit yourself. Mobile homes are not
very mobile, and people who live in them tend to
stay just as put as people in ordinary houses.

The most exciting fact about mobile homes is this: in 1972 they were costing an average of about $6,500 —furnished. This at a time when the average* selling price of a site-built, unfurnished single-family house was about $26,000.

Why this enormous difference? For one thing, the price of the mobile home does not include land and site development. For another, conventional houses are on the average much larger.

But even when the units are the same size, mobiles cost hardly more than half as much as conventional houses—$8 to $10 for each square foot of living space (carpeting, draperies, and furnishings included) compared to at least $16.

It appears that the economies inherent in full factory construction may lead to even lower prices in the future for the mobile units. And we all know where costs of conventional houses have been heading, year after year.

There's a tax advantage, too. So far—but subject to likelihood of change in the near future —mobiles have been taxed gently—as vehicles—instead of brutally—as real estate.

---

* For those who rightly want to be sure we're making a fair and revealing comparison, note that these averages are both for 1972 and both are medians. That is, in each case half the units cost less, and half more, than the figure given here.

A good deal of the (large) difference in price tag between mobile and ordinary homes is accounted for by the land that goes with the latter.

With comparative costs like these, it would appear that the mobile route is the way to go for anyone who must watch his housing dollars. But there is more to the story. There are three financial drawbacks to mobile-home buying.

1. Mobile homes depreciate fast. Just as they are commonly licensed much like motor vehicles, they depreciate almost as fast as autos do. Even in our inflationary times, mobiles have been losing half their market value in the first 6½ years. After that the value drops more slowly until, by the time about 15 years have gone by, they are worth one-fifth to one-third their original cost. (Regular houses, as you know, have tended in our time to appreciate in value instead of losing; and this trend has shown no signs of being near an end.)

Mobile homes are taxed much more lightly
than a home firmly anchored to, and part of, land.

2. Most mobiles are financed at automobile interest rates—10 to 12% when home mortgages are going
at 7 or 7½%. (But FHA and VA financing is now
offered for some mobiles, at normal home-mortgage
rates.)

3. When you buy a house you are investing in land,
which can be expected to increase in value year after
year. As a mobile-park dweller you rent the use of
land and cannot expect to share in the appreciation in
value. (But if you buy a lot for your mobile home on

your own or in a mobile-home subdivision, you eliminate this disadvantage.)

The only honest conclusion from this is that a mobile home offers no clear-cut, over-all financial advantage over other kinds of housing. To find out whether
it does for you, you will have to do some investigating
and adding up of figures and alternatives. Here is the
pattern, as one family found it. Let's call them the
Wrights.

Mobiles vs. others in dollars

They first looked at the newest mobile models.
They found these average 12 feet wide by 60 feet long.
Much larger are the houses formed by putting two
or even three basic units side by side. They chose a
"doublewide" costing about $10,000. (Half the units
sold in California are "doublewides," they learned.)

This could be purchased for 20% down and payments spread over 7 years at 10% interest. Their payments would be $132.81 a month, according to a
standard mortgage-loan payment table. Since there
are 84 monthly payments in 7 years, and $8,000 ÷ 84
= $95.24, they could find their average monthly
interest payment by subtracting $95.24 from $132.81.

Rent for space in the trailer park that they favored
would be $60 a month for the unit in question.

From residents in the park they learned that they
could expect to pay a relatively modest $200 a year
vehicle and personal-property tax. There would be no
ordinary county or city property tax, of course, except

to the extent that one of the things their site rental was calculated to cover was a portion of the property tax paid by the owner of the land on which the trailer park sat.

They were also able to make some reasonably good estimates of maintenance, heating and other utility bills, and insurance costs by talking to owners of units similar to the one they were considering.

Since interest and most taxes are deductible for income-tax purposes, the Wrights added these together ($37.57 + $16.67 = $54.24). Since they were in the 25% bracket for income tax, they took 25% of this amount as their average monthly tax saving resulting from purchase and ownership of the mobile home.

(Actual saving would be more than this in early years, when nearly half each monthly payment would be for interest, and less in the later years of the loan.)

Paying off in seven years

Then they made a similar list of costs for owning a house they considered comparable in living qualities to the mobile home. They did this for the 7-year period in which the mobile would be paid off. Although it was only slightly larger than the mobile, the selling price of this house was more than twice as much, because it included land and involved a construction cost per square foot about double that of the factory-built mobile. Its price came to $24,000, of which they estimated $4,000 represented value of the site.

Beginning with the same amount of cash, $2,000—to keep costs as comparable as possible—they would require a mortgage of nearly $22,500. The extra $500 was for closing costs, not involved in a mobile-home purchase, and furnishings they would need in a new house but not in a pre-furnished mobile.

At 7¼%, a 30-year $22,500 mortgage requires monthly payments of $153.49. Since very little goes toward principal in the early years of a long-term mortgage, they estimated that about $130 of this would be for interest, on the average, during those initial 7 years.

Rent, no; taxes, yes

Where as owners of a mobile home they would have monthly site rent, as house buyers they would have none. But in a typical town or city their taxes as homeowners would be much higher; in this instance about $600, as they learned from owners of a house similar to the one they were contemplating.

For maintenance-utilities-insurance, they estimated an average monthly cost of $75, compared with $50 for the mobile home.

They added their estimated monthly property tax cost ($50) to the figure for mortgage interest ($130) to find they'd have $180 a month to deduct from income for income-tax purposes—a net saving of about $45 a month for people in their 25% bracket.

With the same initial expense, the comparison for monthly costs worked out like this.

MONTHLY COSTS	$10,000 mobile	$24,000 house
loan repayment and interest	132.81	153.49
park rent	60.00	——
taxes	16.67	50.00
maintenance, utilities, insurance	50.00	75.00
TOTAL	259.48	278.49
income tax saving	13.56	45.00
NET COST	245.92	234.49

The first thing our researching family concluded from these figures is that, for housing of comparable size, monthly costs would be pretty much the same. Although the conventional house came out slightly ahead in the tabulation, this was made true only by the greater income tax saving. In any year in which it was no more costly to take the standard deduction in filing their federal return, they would be somewhat ahead with a mobile home.

Like all taxpayers, the Wrights could either list and deduct from taxable income such things as interest and property and sales taxes paid and most medical costs and charitable contributions—or they could deduct a flat amount based on a percentage of their income up to a maximum. Deductible expenses produce a saving only to the extent that all of them together add up to more than the standard deduction would be.

They also noted that by dropping to an ordinary, smaller mobile home they could reduce their net cost for most items about 60%—the natural consequence of buying a $6,000 home instead of a $10,000 one. This could cut their outlay per month to as little as about $170. Among single-family houses it might be difficult to find anything to buy that was that much smaller and cheaper and in an acceptable neighborhood.

Being forward-looking people, the Wright family then went on to consider the position in which they would find themselves after 7 years.

If they bought a mobile home it would then be fully paid for, and their expenses would instantly drop by $123.42 a month ($132.81 loan payments ended, but $9.39 tax saving lost). If they had bought a house instead, the payments would go on for 23 more years, unless they sold it and moved about that time.

Since that is actually the more realistic way to look at it—the average American family moves at least that often—our people finally zeroed in on the most helpful comparison of all.

Where, they asked, will we stand 7 years from now? With mobile homes ordinarily depreciating 50% in the first 6½ years, it is clear that they would be full owners of a unit worth about $5,000.

On the conventional house, the Wrights would have paid some $1,900 on the principal in 7 years. How much their actual equity would be worth would depend upon how the real-estate market in their locality had behaved. In a prospering locality, experience over recent years would indicate, their equity would have grown by well over $5,000—helped primarily by inflation in general and the rapid increase in land values.

But that's clearly a gamble. And the economic aspect remains something of a toss-up. The Wrights could make their decision on the basis of what they really preferred to do, without feeling unthrifty.

CHAPTER IV

Checking Out
a House

Having just completed the sale of our former home, I can tell you one sad thing: Unless you examine your prospective home with far greater shrewdness and expertise than 90% of the would-be buyers we met, only good luck can save you from a poor choice.

Most of the people who came to view our house had no idea what to look for. They concentrated on essentially meaningless details—condition of kitchen equipment, cedar lining in a closet, a charming little light fixture—involving a handful of dollars. No one took a close look at the foundation, few asked about insulation and wall structure and sewer arrangements or tested functioning of plumbing devices.

The fact is that looking for a house calls for some study and preparation, like any other worthwhile art. This should begin with a little self-study, an examination of your family and how it functions and may want to function in the future.

This is one of the first things an architect would do with you if he were designing a house for your family; it is at least as important when you are choosing an existing one.

A study made at the Pratt Institute School of Architecture tells us how families change as years go by. During the first 5 years of marriage, a one-bedroom house or studio apartment is adequate for most people. During the second 5 years, as income grows and children are added, the need changes to a 2- or 3-bedroom home with more storage and living space. During the third 5 years still more living space is needed, with more bedrooms and an additional bathroom or two. In the fourth and fifth 5-year periods needs are stabilized but there may be a change to another city for job reasons or to a better quality home because of increased income. In the sixth, seventh, and eighth 5-year periods, needs dwindle rapidly and a large home may become a liability. Yet it is just at this time that so many families buy too-large, too-expensive homes.

You should not only inspect very carefully
before buying but also write down what you find.

In what respects is your present home unsatis-
factory? When a home-finance agency polled more
than a thousand families, these reasons for house-
shopping topped the list.
1. Rooms too small.
2. Not enough storage space.
3. Poor laundry facilities.
4. Inconvenient and awkward room arrangement.
5. Bedrooms too small for comfortable furniture
   arrangement.
6. Not enough eating or working space in the
   kitchen.

> Begin your own personal housing study with a similar critique of your present arrangements.

Consider such possible items as: neighborhood has become too noisy; need a garage big enough for two cars plus a workshop; need separate quarters for mother-in-law; would like a fireplace.

No need to make the list short. With a full and realistic understanding of why you're planning a change and what you want, you're ready to start looking seriously and effectively.

First, you need to get leads.

Begin by reading newspaper classified advertising. This is not only one of the best ways to find a suitable house but also a good background source on what's available in the area and for how much.

Is the owner obligated?

Ads will lead you directly to owners, who are offering their houses themselves, as well as to real-estate offices. In general, if you are a canny looker you'll save money by dealing directly with an owner since real-estate commissions average around 6% of selling price, as noted earlier. But be sure the owner is not obligated to a real-estate firm. If he has given an exclusive listing he will have to pay full commission and probably will allow for this in his price.

Buying through a salesman is the easier way. Skilled, conscientious salesmen can and have saved many an inexperienced buyer from a costly mistake. Some real-estate people call themselves "Realtors," which means they are members of a national association pledged to a code of ethics. However, since policing of ethical standards is left to local boards which may be more interested in the happiness of their members than in that of clients, you may find—as I have—that this is no guarantee at all.

Tour the neighborhoods

A third major source of possible buys—some subject to commission, others not—is a tour of likely neighborhoods with an eye peeled for FOR SALE signs. In some areas real-estate firms are forbidden to post such signs but owners may do so—and they seldom overlook this opportunity unless they have decided to deal only through an agency.

There will be "open houses" on week ends, and guide signs so you can find them. Some houses-for-sale are shown by appointment only. A real-estate broker can make an appointment or you can phone for one.

Check bulletin boards at your office, club, super-market. Large companies and military bases have housing offices which list available properties, many of which come on the market because of job transfers.

Even the obituary column can be a tip-off to a potential house buy. Heirs who live far away may need cash, not a house.

Newspapers list auctions and bidding-by-mail estate sales of homes. A property of this kind will be open for inspection prior to sale. Highest bidder among those submitting a sealed bid by a specified date gets the house.

What if you admire a house that is not for sale? Knock on the door. Ask the occupant if he is interested in selling. Real-estate brokers do this sometimes when they need more listings. If the owner doesn't want to sell he is usually flattered enough to show you the home and tell you the name of the builder or architect, should you decide to build a similar house.

Where is it located?

While you're getting leads, bear in mind *location*. Choice of a first-rate location is of primary importance for you now as a homebuyer, as well as for that future day when you might want to sell.

It may take some sleuthing to find out why one house is low in price and another, maybe across the street, is much higher. Every area has dividing lines. Which side of the street you're on may determine whether your children go to a convenient, new, well-

The real estate pages of the newspaper tell you
who is selling; the obituary section
indicates who has just vacated a house.

run school or to an inferior one in a distant part of
town. A house on one block may have city sewer,
fire and police protection, garbage collection, and
free library service. Another house, not 50 feet away,
may be outside city limits and have none of these
facilities.

You can't assume that the real-estate broker or
owner will fill you in on all these details. The owner
may have no children and know nothing about the
schools. A real-estate broker who never cracks a book

A case of an "improvement" begun in the area
after the house has been sold to someone
who didn't know what was coming.

will consider library availability unimportant in a decision to purchase a house.

Since it's up to you to judge the location, start by getting a map of the area, one that shows city boundary lines, future streets, proposed parks, playgrounds —and freeways, airports, and transportation lines. (That perfect home on a quiet street could become a nightmare huddled under the roar of jets or neighbor to an on-ramp of a new freeway.)

You might even acquire a house with a park in its future. One young couple considering an old house two blocks from the harbor in Newport Beach, Cali-

fornia, were put off by the presence of a weedy vacant lot across the street. Worse, they could imagine it eventually giving birth to a structure that would cut off their ocean view.

But a wise visit to city hall revealed that the lot belonged to the city and was destined to become a mini-park. The improvement shortly took place and added both pleasure and many dollars of potential resale value to the young couple's home.

You will of course be looking at more than one house and, to be systematic in your looking, you should work with checklists.

In the appendix you will find checklists covering more than a hundred of the most important things to look for when judging a house. Not every item will apply to all houses, of course, because the answers to some of them make others irrelevant. Nor will all of them be relevant to you. Consider the items on the lists as reminders of things to look for and judge their importance to you by the standards of your own family makeup, habits, needs.

Along with rules and tips that apply to all houses, you'll find a special check list for brand-new houses. The unused house, especially when it is part of a tract or subdivision or development, offers some special buying hazards of its own. As with cars and other merchandise, the house that has never been used may be loaded with design flaws, assembly errors, poor construction, faulty materials, "bugs" that are possibly uncorrectable, even outright fraud.

When nearly new $50,000 houses began sliding down California hills a few winters ago, many owners found that although the fault was not theirs the loss was.

Some had the homes rebuilt, adding safety precautions. Others sold out for whatever they could get. All know now the danger of buying a house built on fill where roads have been sliced into hills above and there is no ground cover or trees to hold the earth in place if heavy rain comes too soon.

What's the builder's reputation?

The new house you look at may be an individually built, speculative venture of a small builder. Or it may be a model house, a sample of many being put up by a developer. Either way, the best single short cut you have in judging its quality is the reputation of the builder. So it is with him that you'll find the new-home checklist beginning.

CHAPTER V

Older Houses and Antiques

On the real-estate market, at least, there is no such thing as an old house.* If it isn't new or newish or nearly new, or possibly middle-aged, it is an "older home." This doesn't sound as old as "old" does.

And if a house is very old it is an antique, a description calculated to add greatly to its value—or anyway its price.

Not all wines or all houses age well. Some houses just keep on getting older and weaker and less desirable, deteriorating along with their neighborhoods; if they are good buys it is only because the price is

---

* Just as there is no such thing any more as a row house. Now if the house you own shares walls with a neighbor, you are living in a condominium—or in a "town house," even if it is in the country.

64

low. Others, although unoccupied, with windows broken, porches sagging, surrounded by slums, may suddenly become "antiques"—and valuable.

This is true especially of large, old, well-built Victorian houses. In their heyday no expense was spared to make them showpieces—hand-carved staircases, solid hardwood floors and woodwork, handmade cabinets and filigree, imported stained-glass windows, large rooms and plenty of them. Wherever they exist, Victorian houses are being snapped up at low prices, to be restored at high cost. They're worth it, provided the neighborhood in which they stand is also being updated.

Bargains in slums

Some 1600 families, from New York to Florida, applied for the privilege of being purchasers of one of the 125 houses in an Oakland slum. Word got around that these Victorian homes, hand-built by sailors around 1900, were to be sold at prices from $4,500 to $6,000.* The US government agency, HUD, will loan a buyer as much as $17,000 to restore one of the single-family units, as much as $34,800 to restore a 2-family home. The down payment on these houses was set at less than $2,000. All a buyer had to do was take possession and start restoration. When

---

* Most 19th century ships were made largely of wood, demanding expert maintenance, so carried able carpenters. Many found employment in seaport areas during idle periods ashore, using their talents for housebuilding. They came from many parts of the world, took great pride in their work, and produced structures with fine detailing unrivaled today.

A genuine Victorian house can be a good buy.
They built solidly in those days.

completed he would have a house worth from
$20,000 to $40,000.

Already 200 houses in Oakland have been restored,
and the city is cooperating by repairing streets and
sidewalks as well as putting power lines underground.

Another section of this same city has 500 Victorian
houses, of which about half have now been restored. This situation is being repeated in many areas
of the country. Nearly all cities, especially those near
seaports, have possibilities for the antique-home
seeker.

Of course not every older house, or every antique one, is a bargain. You should judge your
prospective purchase harshly, using such rules
as those that follow. Apply also the hundred-

odd tips in the appendix checklist on judging houses. As they stand, few older houses will meet any of these tests. But use them to judge the desirability and suitability of the house you see yourself turning it into.

Above all, get realistic figures—firm ones where possible—on those improvements that will be needed before that old house meets your standards of today.

1. First of all, you are buying location. Is the house in an area that is being generally renewed or is it an isolated mansion in a slum that will continue to be a slum? Will the area become completely industrial? Ask about zoning at city hall.

2. How much will it really cost in dollars and cents? The buying price is the least of your expenditures. An

old house may have to be rebuilt from plumbing to roof. Find out what other comparable restorations have cost, how difficult the jobs were, whether the owners have succeeded in doing any of the work themselves. Will you need an architect?

3. Very old houses tend to be close to noisy business districts. Could you put up with heavy traffic, a crowded neighborhood, bars, restaurants, and little open space around you?

4. Transportation and public facilities will probably be close, but don't take their convenience and quality for granted. Test them yourself.

5. How are the schools? If they exist, are they also unrestored, ugly, and inefficient? Will your children have to battle heavy business traffic to get to them? If no schools are near, will your youngsters have to be transported to a school in a distant residential district?

6. What kinds of conversions will zoning laws permit? With so much space you may start to plan a duplex or a unit apartment, only to find that zoning laws forbid it. One good buy in some cities is a big old house near the campus of a university. Zoning regulations permitting, you could create an elegant home in such a neighborhood, turning excess space into apartments to rent to students and teachers.

7. What about taxes? Will they shoot up as you add to value? Will you be taxed as a business property? Or will you perhaps get a special tax break? Some cities are giving bonuses to property owners who restore antique houses.

The old French Quarter of New Orleans was renewed with the aid of highly favorable tax breaks for persons who agreed to restore under specific regulations. Apartments in the French Quarter are now so much in demand they are "handed down" and rarely come on the open rental or purchase market.

8. What about other types of restoration possibilities? The old barn? The carriage house? The abandoned windmill? The gate house on a large estate? Any of these can be bargains.

9. Consider the drawbacks. Expect to spend many times the original price, plus a good deal of your own time and energy in decisions and work. If you live in the house while it's being restored, remember you will be inhabiting a slum made up of dust, dirt, a parade of workmen, and inferior living space until the project is completed—sometimes a matter of years. If you rent other housing while the restoration is going on, count that cost as restoration expense, too.

10. Be realistic about how much value will be added by major improvements. Aside from your personal use, certain additions will pay off on resale, while others usually will not.

Except for its value to your family, adding either a swimming pool or a large patio or finishing an attic or basement room is more debatable. Not every buyer wants these features. And what is not wanted may be an actual liability. Even if the cost of the improvement is not included in your selling price, a buyer will think it is.

That's why those expensive bomb shelters built a decade ago often go unmentioned when a salesman shows a house today.

CHAPTER VI

The Custom House: Making a Dream Come True

It's the expensive way to go—having a house built to your own specifications.

But it may be worth it to you, especially if you simply cannot find the combination of location, surroundings, plan, size, and style that you want in an existing house.

It's the expensive way because: You are in effect buying your lot at retail instead of wholesale as a developer does. You are missing out on all the economies in material purchase and labor costs that come with mass production of houses.

Your dream house may turn out to be just
that if your desires are quite special.

Also, your house must carry a heavy share of a small builder's overhead and profit. You must pay full price for landscaping and a host of extras, if you want them, that often come with a used house at little extra cost.

And this single house must bear the cost of a design into which many hours of talent and skill may have gone.

Having made a dream house appear as extravagant as—in sad truth—it very often is, let's take a look at some ways around this obstacle.

Cal and Midge Mason are about to build a new home for themselves and young Mark, who is 7. They know what they want—pretty much—and they have already searched their town in vain for anything like it.

"No wonder!" Midge sighs. "If I had a house like the one I'm dreaming about I wouldn't part with it either."

Having consulted one architect, several real-estate salesmen, and a couple of excellent custom builders, the Masons have learned that a house of the size and quality they have in mind will come to about $55,000 in their rather expensive small city.

The arithmetic behind that price is simple. The least-expensive suitable lots the Masons have been shown were listed at $11,000. They want a house of about 1,600 square feet, and the going rate for custom construction is at least $25 a square foot in their area. That comes to $40,000. Few architects will design a small house and supervise its construction for a fee of less than 10%; $4,000 in this case, of which the design alone accounts for perhaps $2,400.

Before deciding what to do, Cal and Midge list the parts that make up that awesome $55,000, using round numbers:

Land: $11,000.

Design: $2,400.

Supervision: architect, $1,600; time, overhead, and profit for contractor and sub-contractors, $10,000; total $11,600.

On-site labor (carpenters, plumbers, etc.): $15,000.

Materials: $15,000.

For that amount of money—$55,000—the Masons know, they could have just the house they wanted built for them—and with the least effort for them. They need only choose their architect well and make certain that they fully communicate to him their needs and means and desires.

The architect would help them select their lot. He would talk to them at length. He would draw a complete and highly detailed sheaf of plans and specifications for them—first, perhaps, submitting rough sketches and preliminary ideas.

They can be reasonably confident that the plan finally chosen will fit not only their wishes but also their lot and—although this is less certain—their pocketbook as described to the architect in their first session.

Some friends of the Masons have become home-owners by this route and today, a year later, remain proud and happy about the whole thing, although slightly dazed at the way costs got out of hand somewhere in the process.

It's costs that shatter the dream houses of most people.

The Masons are tempted to follow this example, except they hope to keep costs down on those extras. But they can see that, although the down payment is within possibility, the monthly mortgage payments would be a critically dangerous undertaking. As there is more than one way to skin a cat, so with building a house. The Masons see that for them it will have to be a different way from that of their better-heeled friends.

Their first move is to start at the top of their cost list, with land.

"If we can buy a lot directly from the owner, we can probably at least save the amount of the commission," Midge points out. "And around here that's a flat 10% on vacant land."

This decision means touring the area in which they are interested, looking for vacant lots that fit their specifications, noting their location. It means identifying them on tax maps at city hall or county court house, obtaining names and addresses of owners from tax records, and phoning or writing to find out if the owners are interested in selling.

This procedure, definitely time-consuming but enjoyable on the whole, will ordinarily turn up a lot at a considerable saving. For the Masons it produced two that are just about what they have in mind—and one that slopes sharply down from the street.

"Looks like we can buy one or the other of the level lots for $9,500 or so," Cal concludes. "Or the steep one for a couple thousand less . . . which from what I read is about what it would cost extra to build on it."

So, either way, the Masons' saving from their do-it-yourself land buying approach should come to about $1,500. A good beginning but hardly decisive.

How can the Masons save on the next item, design? They can skip the architect they had in mind, going instead to an architectural student or a recent graduate who is unemployed or moonlighting, or to a designer who is not a full-fledged architect. Such people can be very good indeed, but the rule holds that you get no more than you pay for, and the risks in this course are obvious. Midge and Cal decline to take them.

"No," says Midge. "If I had a little more courage and a little more experience, I'd design it myself if necessary and pay a good architectural draftsman to handle the details. Maybe someday . . . .

"But now I think we should study all the sources of ready-drawn plans that we can be confident of. The home magazines offer complete sets of plans, for $35 or $50 or so, that have been drawn for clients who paid a lot of money for them. If we can find one that fits us and our lot, we'll get for a few dollars plans that have thousands of dollars worth of talent invested in them."

Midge's idea is good, but it is not without its flaws. For one thing, they will need good judgment in choosing a plan, especially if their building site is not a typical one. They may encounter some problems, and require local architectural assistance, if the building code in their area differs from the one where the architect of their chosen plan works. And if they find a plan they like only in part and try to adapt it they are in danger of coming out with an unworkable hybrid.

If the Masons do come up with a satisfactory stock plan, they will be the logical ones to supervise construction. In saving part of the architect's fee, they might as well go all the way and save the rest.

Whether Midge and Cal can safely save more of the supervision costs by acting as their own general contractor will depend upon how much experience they have had with building. This would mean they would themselves hire workmen to do any or all of the parts of construction—concrete work, framing, finish carpentry, plumbing, wiring—instead of having a general contractor subcontract the work.

If the Masons go this far—finding their own lot and bargaining with the owner for it, drawing their own plan or digging till they find a good enough one ready-made, then supervising all construction—they stand to save as much as $15,000 or so. Their hopelessly expensive dream house may come in for as little as an entirely feasible $40,000.

It may not work out as well as that, of course. Cal or Midge, or both of them, may lose interest midway through the project. Or they may simply find themselves out of their depth—more confident than competent.

It is a fact that each year many thousands of families undertake to build their own houses in every respect except the actual building labor. Some succeed very well. Others fail expensively. We can only hope that Cal and Midge are good judges of their own capacity and do not undertake more than they can handle.

With their own hands

We should add that as moneysavers, the Masons are by no means going all the way. Millions of Americans, many with little previous construction experience, have built their own houses in the most literal sense. That is, they have built them with their own hands, personally doing all or a major part of the carpentry, plumbing, roofing, wiring, cabinetwork, and finishing.

Personally building your own home is not for everyone, any more than sailing or deep-sea diving or landscape painting is. But for those to whom the idea really appeals, it constitutes an enterprise of enormous interest and, of course, profit. We'll come to this subject later.

CHAPTER VII

The Money Trap: 1. Mortgages

In the early pages of this book the case of the Husers and Uncle Jim warned us that it can be financially dangerous to buy a house—and financially foolish not to.

In the words of the old song, "It ain't whatcha do, it's the way you do it." That's what this and the next chapter deal with: ways to handle the financial side of home building and buying—and ways not to. In short, the home mortgage, its many variations, and its alternatives, good and bad.

The basic and most usual kind of mortgage arrangement is called a conventional home loan. After making a down payment you borrow enough from a bank or savings-and-loan company, or perhaps a mortgage or insurance company or private lender, to pay the rest of the cost of the house.

You pay off this indebtedness in equal monthly payments over a period of 20 to 25 years, occasionally more or less. Then the house becomes yours.

Each payment covers the interest you owe for one month and also makes a small dent in the principal amount. Over the years, as the size of the mortgage dwindles, less interest is required each month and more goes toward the principal; and only at about that time will you find that you still owe as much as you have paid off.

Another sobering fact—and one rarely recognized—is this: interest more than doubles the cost of a typical house purchase. A 30-year loan at 7½% interest will require payments totaling more than $250 for each $100 of the original amount. That is, you will pay $1.50 interest as well as $1 in repayment of principal for each $1 you borrow.

In spite of what you have heard all these years, the most costly purchase you'll ever make is probably not your new home—it's the mortgage on it. A $25,000 home loan at 8% for 30 years will cost you a (truly) grand total of $41,038 in interest alone. Those monthly payments of $183 you'll be making for 360 months come to $66,038. Even with a 20-year loan at 8%, the total you'll repay will be somewhat more than twice the amount you have borrowed.

Don't be surprised if the mortgage costs more than the house.

That's one overwhelming reason why the terms of your home loan are worthy of your closest attention.

Carefully shop, shrewdly argue

The other reason is that these terms are almost as variable as the colors and floor plans of the houses that carry them. The terms you commit yourself to for many years to come will depend upon how carefully you shop around and how shrewdly you argue and compare.

At all times except those rare periods when money is extremely tight, various banks and insurance companies as well as savings-and-loan organizations are hotly competing to sell you a loan. Take advantage of this competition to land yourself the mortgage best suited to your unique needs at the lowest price the market offers.

Following are the factors to look for, ask about, and weigh in shopping for the mostest for the leastest in mortgage money. The essentials are the same whether the arrangement is called a mortgage or, as in some areas, a deed of trust.

What kind of loan is it?

Home loans divide into two main types: government sponsored and conventional. In most areas the latter kind are more usual today, except where groups of houses are involved.

At the top of the list

Best of all are the subsidized kind. If your state has such a program (in California it's called Calvet, for veterans) and you're eligible, it can save you a lot of money. VA (sometimes called GI) or Veterans Administration loans are also something of a bargain for those who qualify through military service. The government guarantees them up to $12,500 (or 65% if that's less) and they are often made with little or nothing down when the appraiser agrees that the house is worth the full selling price.

Next best is an FHA loan, which is insured—but not subsidized by the government, specifically the Federal Housing Administration. This insurance will cost you an added ½%. Be sure to include this cost in your comparisons. Although the government guarantees FHA loans, it does not make them; banks and other lending institutions do.

In many areas the great majority of home loans made by banks and savings and loans are the kind called conventional. That is, they have no government guarantees or subsidies. Even conventional loans may vary startlingly from one bank or S&L to the next—in respect to interest rates charged, amount of loan offered, and subsidiary clauses.

There are private mortgage-insurance agencies as well as government ones. They include Mortgage

Guarantee Insurance Corporation (known as MGIC), American Mortgage Insurance Corporation, and Continental Mortgage Insurance, Inc.

Here is how this kind of insurance might make it possible for you to buy a house. You have found just what you want at $20,000, but can manage only 10% down. After having been unable to get either a conventional or FHA loan for the needed $18,000, you find a savings and loan that will provide it if an insurance company will cover most of the risk.

Different lenders will offer different amounts in mortgage money—and at different times.

MGIC or equivalent insurance is obtained. The cost (paid by you, of course) is a $20 appraisal-review fee plus a first-year cost of ½ of 1% of the amount of the loan. For these fees, MGIC will guarantee the top 20% of your loan, which is $3,600. The lender is risking only $14,400. On a $20,000 house this is a pretty safe loan, so he is happy to make it.

Your loan-insurance premium will decrease each year. You may even be able to persuade the lender to drop it after a few years as the loan becomes smaller and your reputation as a reliable payment-maker grows.

Can you get a large enough loan?

Banks often lend a severely limited percentage of the appraised value of the property, perhaps as little as 65% to 75% of the value unless the loan is insured. Savings and loan banks and mortgage companies may go much higher; many are embracing a new plan that lets them finance up to 95%.

Banks' appraisal policies and their restrictions on what kind of property they will lend on can be more conservative, too. Rules for determining your financial capacity for a given loan are also something that may vary among institutions. One loan officer will consider your wife's job permanent, while another will discount its importance on an assumption it may prove temporary. A private lender may be most flexible of all, although likely to require a relatively high rate of interest, unless he is the seller of the house.

If the FHA is to insure the loan you get from a bank or other institution, you must qualify under rather rigid rules. Since most lenders observe much the same policies, it will be helpful to you in your dealings to know what they are.

To begin with, you must show that you have a dependable income. A second income in the family will count only if it comes from what appears to be a permanent job. Such sources of income as casual moonlighting or overtime work, plans to rent out a room in the new house—these may not count at all, even though they loom large in your own financial planning.

Your income vs. your living standards

Your standard of living must appear to be within your income; and your indebtedness and general credit rating must reflect this.

Your total financial obligations must leave room for the new payments. Everything else being equal, if you have children approaching college age you will be considered to be in a more demanding financial period than if they were very young or already through school. You will not be encouraged to take heavy risks or make excessive sacrifices in order to buy a house.

Your total housing expenses will be considered, including payments, taxes, insurance, maintenance, repairs, utilities, and even transportation if this is influenced by the location. If this total is substantially larger than your present total costs, and you have not been able to save any money in the past, this will weigh against you.

All these factors will be put together along with a few others: age (30–40 is excellent, 25–29 good, 41–55 fair, over 55 or under 25 poor); number of dependents (1 or 2 children favored); life insurance (highest rating if you carry twice the amount of the proposed mortgage).

What's the interest rate?

Like the price of anything else you buy, this does vary. Not only from week to week but also from one lender to another not a block away.

The fees can vary, too

Banks traditionally charge a little less than other institutions except insurance companies. When all have identical rates, note that fees and costs for making the loan vary, as noted below.

Examples of how rates may vary:

A friend of mine saved substantially on a new home loan early in 1972 by discovering that although the rate at his bank had gone up the previous week to

7¼%, another bank which he dealt with was still holding firm at 7. He closed the deal just hours before his bank branch received orders from headquarters to go up.

A prejudice against writers

When mortgaging our old home eight years ago to get money to build a new one, I found four rates offered by standard lending institutions within a radius of a few miles. Savings and loans wanted 6¼%; one branch bank serving a wealthy residential area loaded with big depositors, 5¾%; a big insurance company, 5½%. Having grabbed the 5¾% I've been saving $5 to $10 a month ever since. (I couldn't save the other ¼% because the insurance company wouldn't have me. At their much-in-demand bargain rate they could afford to be fussy, and writers don't have sufficiently steady income to be prime risks, they told me*.)

How important to you is a jump from 7%, say, to 8%? For a typical mortgage (rate 6% to 9%, term 20–30 years) each jump will add $6 to $7 to each monthly payment for each $10,000 of mortgage debt.

* A 25-year-veteran free-lance writer has a more dependable income than most people, I told them: nobody can fire him. They didn't agree.

Here's another way to assay it. If through unfortunate circumstances or bad timing or careless choice of lender, you find yourself paying 8% when it might have been 7%, it will take you 25 years to pay off what otherwise could have been a 20-year loan at the same monthly cost. Figured this way, the higher rate will eventually have added roughly $9,200 to the payoff cost of a $20,000 loan. The price of a couple of new cars or a luxurious trip around the world for two.

It pays to look carefully, ask around, and bargain hard for the lowest available price when you are buying money just as when buying anything else, especially since it's the largest purchase a family makes in a lifetime.

Is it a variable-rate mortgage?

This is the newest thing—still uncommon but possibly soon to be the usual thing. It is a logical idea but it can be very much to your financial disadvantage, so it is essential to know what it's all about.

Going up, going down

As you might guess, it is a mortgage on which the interest rate (and your monthly payments) can go up or down with changes in the prevailing rate. It may be provided that this adjustment is to be made at 5-year intervals.

If you are confident that interest rates are going to drop generally in the future, you will like the variable idea. If you think you are getting in at a relatively low period, you will fight to stay away from such a thing.

Here is how a variable might work. Suppose you were to take out a variable 8% 30-year mortgage today for $25,000. Monthly payments would be about $183.

If after the specified interval, perhaps 5 years, the going rate had risen to 8½%, your payments would then go up to $191 a month. If the rate should rise to 9% after another 5 years your payments would go up to $198.

A drop to 7½%, however, after the first 5 years would reduce your payments to $176. If another 5 years saw interest rates declining to 7% your payments would shrink to a pleasant $169.

Watch out for points

In general you should prefer to avoid the variable feature. When rates go up, this feature hurts you. When rates go down a little, it helps you—a little. When rates go down sharply, you already have protection—you can escape by refinancing, as described in the following chapter on mortgage management. So you don't really need it, although it might save you a modest amount in new-loan costs.

Any points?

These are a rather mysterious extra charge in the form of an additional loan fee. A bank or other lender may charge you one or more points for your loan when he is not willing to make it at the stated interest rate but finds it awkward (or forbidden, in the case of an FHA rate fixed by law) to raise it directly.

"Point" is short for percentage point. But it refers to a charge you have to pay only once, not every year. "We can give you a mortgage for $22,000," says the lender, "but you'll have to pay 2 points." That means you pay a one-time charge of 2% of the $22,000, or $400, in addition to any other loan fees and closing costs.

In the case of an FHA loan, which is the type most often involving points, the law forbids charging the buyer points directly. The seller may pay points, however. And when he does it is likely that they will find their way into the selling price of the house.

Points and mortgage life

Since points are essentially a way of raising the interest rate on a mortgage to bring it into line with the market value of mortgage money, it is important to know just how much effect they have. This depends on the life of the mortgage—not just the stated life but how long you actually pay on it before selling out or retiring it.

Look at it this way. If you retire the mortgage for some reason at the end of a single year (perhaps selling the house to a cash buyer), 2 points will have cost you an additional 2%. Your 7% mortgage will have cost you about 9%. But if you spread the cost of those 2 points over 20 or 30 years of mortgage payments, they will have cost you only a fraction of 1% each year.

How to figure a point

A good rule of thumb to judge by is this: assuming you keep the mortgage until 20-year maturity, each point is the equivalent of ⅛ of a percentage point added to the stated rate of interest.

So when you hold a 20-year mortgage at 7% plus 4 points all the way to maturity its cost to you is approximately the same as for a 7½% loan with no points.

Is there a prepayment penalty?

After a lender has gone to the trouble of making a loan, he doesn't want it paid off before he has had time to collect quite a bit of interest. Also, since he's in the position of having to keep the loan in force at a fixed interest rate no matter where the money market goes, he doesn't want you to be able to pay him off by borrowing elsewhere for less when the going rate slips. So he may stipulate a penalty if you pay ahead.

With a conventional mortgage, terms are negotiable, so try to avoid any penalty. You may want to make bigger payments. Or you may want to sell the house. Or you may want to refinance. Since FHA's discontinuance of prepayment penalties in July 1972 you should find yourself in a better strategic position to fight off such a penalty clause.

Open end?

A very desirable provision that many mortgages will include is one that lets you reborrow money you have paid in. The most desirable type, from your point of view, provides that you may do this at the same interest rate.

Suppose you've been paying on a $25,000, 30-year, 6% mortgage for the last 12 years. The remaining balance is $19,767. You need money for improving your home—or for a child's college or for a trip abroad . . . anything. With an open-end mortgage you can borrow any amount up to the difference between $30,000 and $19,767. Depending upon the agreement, you will repay this $5,233 (plus interest, inevitably) by larger monthly payments or by an extension in the maturity date of the mortgage.

The danger of open-end

Nice thing about open-end is that it does no harm if not used, yet can be extremely convenient if needed. It's a good way to save money. The only drawback is that it may present too much temptation.

Caution—is there a balloon?

A balloon is a whopping great final payment, often in the thousands of dollars. When there is reason to write a home loan for a comparatively short period

A balloon normally is light but a balloon payment
as the final one on a mortgage can break your back.

a final balloon payment is the only way to keep monthly payments low. There is nothing wrong with a balloon in itself, but you must understand what it means and be prepared to meet it.

Although balloon payments often come with mortgages drawn to meet special conditions, they're more likely to be found in conditional sales agreements. So you'll find further discussion of them in the chapter immediately following.

What are the other costs of the loan?

These make up most of what are known as closing costs—those dollars (nearly always in the hundreds, sometimes more than $1,000) you are asked to dig up for expensive incidentals when the final papers are being signed. Depending upon where you live, the nature of the financing, and who is putting up the money, these costs may include most or all of the following: application fee, credit report, survey, title examination, title insurance, attorney fees, origination fee, preparation of documents, closing fee, recording fees, transfer taxes, escrow fees—and, in some areas, a few minor items besides.

Know what you're in for

Since most of these are unavoidable, about all you can do is get a list in advance so you'll know what to be prepared for. If you put all your savings into a down payment, you may be hard put to come up with what may be an unexpectedly large sum for closing costs.

Use this list also in comparing loan sources. When interest rates are the same, your best chance to save may be in this department.

Very often the biggest single cost of closing is for title insurance. As borrower you will be paying for a policy that protects the lender against loss arising from a defect in your title of ownership. Similar pro-

The closing costs for a mortgage loan can
make it difficult to pick up a loan.

tection for you will ordinarily come from a title policy
supplied by the seller—though in some areas it is
customary for buyer to pay for this or to divide cost
with seller. If you find at the time of paying for the
lender's policy that you do not have title insurance
for yourself you can get an owner's policy at the
same time by asking for it and paying perhaps 25%
additional.

What you will pay in closing costs will depend
equally upon how expensive your house is and in
what part of the country you live. For a modest house
in San Antonio, Texas, all these costs may add up to

as little as $11. For an equivalent house in Essex County, N.J., you can expect to put up $585, with title examination and attorney fees the major villains. Those figures are for a house from $12,000 to $20,000. Go to $28,000 and up and the figures become $384 in San Antonio, $843 in Newark.

At closing time you will also be asked to make some other payments. These are normal running costs, but they may come as a shock. They will cover such things as any of your taxes or insurance costs the seller has paid in advance (and so is now entitled to a refund on) and mortgage interest for the interval preceding the period covered by the first regular payment.

Is there an existing mortgage on the property? If there is, find out if the mortgagee will let you assume it. Principal situation in which this may be to your advantage arises when the interest rate it bears is lower than you can get on a new loan. It is not uncommon to find houses for sale with mortgages in the 5–6% range when the lowest available interest on new loans is 7 or even 8%.

The gimmick in the mortgage

The drawback to assumable mortgages is that usually they aren't as big as you'd like and have to be paid off too quickly. Here's an example from a recent sale. The Kramers, a restaurant manager and his wife, found an 8-year-old house they liked very much. Price arrived at after some haggling was $41,000. The existing mortgage, initially $30,000 for 20 years, had been paid down to about $22,000. At a modest 5¾% compared to the going rate of 7½%, it sounded very desirable. The gimmick showed up when Mr. Kramer subtracted $22,000 from $41,000 and realized he'd have to make a $19,000 down payment instead of the $8,200 (20%) one he'd hoped to arrange. Happily, he had enough in investments to dig up the difference, and the bargain interest rate convinced him this was worth doing.

If Mr. Kramer had not had this much cash, he might have been able to interest the seller in taking back a second mortgage for the amount needed. Even if this second were written at a rate somewhat higher than the 7½% current for firsts, the combination would still have been a bargain for Mr. Kramer if he could handle the comparatively high total monthly outlay. His reward would be an early mortgage burning.

Instead of assuming, or taking over, a mortgage, you might buy a house "subject to" an existing loan. This is a perfectly good alternative from the buyer's point of view, but since the seller continues to be responsible instead of fully getting out from under he may not be enthusiastic.

Consider yourself very lucky to find a house
you want with an old—and low-rate—mortgage to take over.

How about a second mortgage?

Caution is called for. The term has an unpleasant ring. It is often associated with high interest rates and buyers who are in over their heads. All the same, there are situations to which a second mortgage can be a legitimate and even economical answer.

One situation justifying a second mortgage, if suitable terms are obtainable, is illustrated by the Kramers in the preceding section. Instead of cashing in investments they might have used a second mortgage to raise the additional down-payment money. They would merely want to ascertain first that they could afford to make the combined monthly payments.

And that is the only safe rule for any buyer: look as sharply at your capacity to pay the combined amount on two mortgages as you would if that total were a monthly payment on a single home loan.

The more usual second is the kind called purchase money. The lender is the seller of the house. He is in effect accepting the down payment partly in cash and partly in a second mortgage in order to sell you the house. If he is eager enough to sell, he may not object to an interest rate no higher than the first mortgage bears. He will not be able to get face value for this second if he has to sell it, but he may feel it is a safe investment for him since he knows intimately the security behind it—the house he's selling.

A seller who is able and willing to take back a second in this manner may be interested in considering a different kind of financing entirely. It's called a contract of sale. With this there is no mortgage, as we will see in the next chapter.

CHAPTER VIII

The Money Trap: 2. Contracts of Sale

Most private sellers of homes want their money now. All of it.

To buy from them you must pay cash—your own, or the proceeds of a loan that you obtain by pledging your new house. But some sellers are prepared to wait (at interest) for some of their money. Such a seller will, as we have seen, "take back a second" for part of the down payment.

Quite often a seller will go even further. Convinced that a mortgage on the house he's selling is a sound investment at a rate of interest similar to that current on first mortgages, he offers you an alternative to a mortgage.

Make a down payment, he says in effect, and owe me the rest. Pay it off to me just as you would to a bank holding a mortgage. When the whole amount has been paid I'll give you title free and clear—just as the bank would at mortgage-burning time.

This arrangement is called a contract of sale. Or a conditional sales contract (meaning the sale is conditional upon your paying the installments). Or an installment sale. Or, very often, a land contract, since it has been most commonly used for sales of land. Such an arrangement, although rarely found in some localities, is possible anywhere. And there are areas where it is the normal thing, perhaps because it may permit a smaller down payment than a mortgage lender could or would permit.

You will recognize this method as similar to the way you might buy a car or a couch, on time payments. The difference is that in the case of real estate there are more safeguards for the buyer. In some states these are equal to those covering mortgages; and in a few, court decisions have made them even more protective.

Before buying a house on a contract of sale rather than a mortgage, consult a lawyer who works with real estate and knows the local rules. Not only can he tell you whether there are any hidden dangers in this arrangement in your state but he can also see that the agreement is drawn up to give you maximum protection should difficulties arise later.

There is one thing above all that you are interested in. It is this: if you are unable to make one or more payments at some time you will not be treated more harshly than you could be under a mortgage agreement.

One advantage of a land contract is that it may permit the seller to postpone, or spread out, payment of some of the income tax on any profit he is making in selling the house. (More about this in the chapter on the tax side of home ownership.) This concerns you because it may offer an incentive to him to accept a lower price in return.

Selling without rules

A second possible advantage to you is that there is no fixed limitation on the size of the down payment. Length of time for the payments to run, rate of interest, and other details may be freely negotiated. A private seller, unlike a lending institution, is not encumbered by rules. Most sellers, however, will expect a rate of interest equal to that obtainable on mortgages at the time. You should make yourself aware what this figure is so that you will not unknowingly pay more.

A third, modest advantage to you is elimination of much of the red tape connected with most real-estate

A seller willing to sell on a contract
rather than a mortgage
saves a buyer closing fees and hassles.

transactions. And with this may vanish many of the
usual irritating closing costs. And since such a sale
as this may or may not be recorded when signed, you
may postpone such things as recording fees and
transfer taxes until the whole amount has been paid
off many years later. If you sell before that happens,
you may never pay them at all.

Where a contract of sale goes unrecorded, still another advantage may appear. In some counties, property-tax authorities keep track of sales and adjust assessed valuations to correspond to selling prices.

The potential danger in leaving a contract of sale unrecorded is that the seller might then—illegally—sell the same property to someone else and then go bankrupt or vanish. So unless there are good reasons not to record and you can trust the seller's honesty and financial soundness, you'd better record.

Balloon payments, mentioned in the chapter on mortgages, often appear in conditional sales contracts. An ordinary seller may be more reluctant than a bank would be to wait 30 years or more for the last of his money . . . especially if he is 60 or so at the time of selling. So a balloon goes in. It may read something like this clause, taken from an agreement entered into by one family, providing for:

"Monthly installments, commencing on July 15, 1972, of $170 or more, including interest at the rate of 7¼% per annum until June 15, 1987, whereupon the entire sum remaining unpaid will become due and payable."

In signing this agreement, the buying family did not assume they would have that whole balance—or even any part of it—sitting by, ready to use, when

1987 inevitably rolled around. They took it for granted they would refinance then, if they still had the house. There is no reason for them to think they will not be able to do this. Their house should be worth more by 1987 and they will owe less on it.

With a contract of sale, as with owner financing through a mortgage, you usually will be dealing with an individual rather than a lending institution. What this means to you may be unpredictable. Institutions generally lean over backwards to avoid foreclosures but an individual may be more demanding. It is equally possible that you would find an individual going further than any bank in liberality in your time of need since he would not be bound by rules.

Remember that rules about contract sales vary so much from state to state that the services of a knowledgeable lawyer are more vital than with a mortgage sale surrounded by established rules.

There have been serious abuses of land contracts in the past. A particularly distressing case was of a seller—a subdivision mass builder—who ran into hard times and decamped with many months of buyers' payments. It turned out that he hadn't been keeping up his own mortgage payments. The buyers lost out even though they had faithfully paid him.

CHAPTER IX

Maintaining and Managing a Mortgage

Once you're convinced the home you covet is good value for the price, your next question naturally is: How much a month?

Tables in the appendix will answer that question for you with a minimum of calculation. These tables give the exact monthly figure for each of the usual interest rates and time-payment periods, for loans of various amounts. They apply equally to conven-

Never, never forget that mortgage payments
fall due regularly and without fail.

tional and guaranteed mortgages and to homes purchased on contract of sale.

To determine whether you can afford a payment of
a given size you must, of course, add other shelter
costs: property taxes, insurance, maintenance. You
may pay these directly, or they may be added to your
basic payments.

Maintenance is the great variable. For people
short of manual skills and interests who have
the misfortune to acquire a house in poor condition, upkeep can be a financial disaster. A
house designed, built, and landscaped for easy
maintenance, on the other hand, may require

only the attention that a willing owner can easily give, at a cost that may average only a few dollars a month.

A typical maintenance chore is replacement of the thermocouple in a gas water heater or furnace, which tends to wear out within 10 years. A new part commonly costs less than $5, and a householder of average savvy can usually install it even if he has never done this particular task before. But put in by a repairman the little thermocouple inevitably is accompanied by a charge of $15 to $25 or so—because the trip alone may have taken up an hour of the repairman's time.

To estimate maintenance costs on your prospective home, begin with a look at history. How much have you (and your landlord, if you've been renting) been spending? How much, if any, more should have been spent for fully adequate maintenance? Judging by the amount of mechanical equipment and its condition, exterior and interior finishes, and status of landscaping, how many times more or less will the new house require? By this route you can arrive at a fairly precise and realistic expectation—and thus avoid a major money trap.

Consider also what is an even bigger figure in many cases: automobile or other daily travel costs to the extent that they will be greater in your new location than in your old.

Many a budget has foundered because that idyllic new setting added 40 miles a day (at 5 to 15 cents a mile) to the daily home-to-job round trip. Other budgets have suffered because the new location virtually isolated the lady of the house until she bought a car of her own.

When you've figured out how much you can afford to pay each month, you don't need to assume that that figure must and will irrevocably remain unchanged during the term of the mortgage. Mortgages can, and should be, managed.

Additional transportation required by a change in dwelling can wreck a family budget.

If you are now carrying a mortgage that was tailored for you two or ten years ago, it is like a suit of clothes of the same age. It may still fit you today—and then again it may not.

It may be uncomfortably tight in its payments or too short in its amortization period. The mortgage may need alterations because your house does. Or

Your old mortgage may not fit you now as well as it did when you first got it. So? So review it and your financial situation from time to time.

you may have a mortgage that was taken out during one of the high-interest periods of recent years when 8%, 9% and even more were the rule.

What may have changed

If so, you may be able to save a surprisingly large amount by refinancing at a lower rate of interest. This saving can be translated into substantially lower monthly payments or into a plan by which the mortgage will be paid off much sooner.

Or yours may be the other of the two general situations in which it may be possible to reduce the cost of an existing mortgage or deed of trust. You may have had to agree to a relatively high rate of interest because your equity was small. If your equity has grown considerably, you may be able to get a lower rate now because the risk to the mortgage holder is reduced. This can have come about in one or more of several ways:

You may have paid off so much of the mortgage that the property now is ample security for the balance.

You may have improved the property so as to increase its value.

Your property may have been in such a remote or undeveloped location that it was regarded as a poor risk. Improvement in the neighborhood may have removed this defect.

Your house or vacation place may have been regarded as too large and expensive to be a good mortgage risk. By the higher housing standards of today this may no longer be true.

Your home may have impressed mortgage people as being too radical in design or construction at the time. "Modern" design, for example, used to frighten bankers much more than it does now.

As a result of one or more of these sequences you may be able to get a new loan at a cheaper rate. As noted in the earlier chapter on mortgages, small changes in rate of interest are far more significant than they may sound. Over the life of a 25-year $20,000 mortgage, reducing the rate from 8½% to 7½% means a whopping $3,975 in your pocket. It cuts monthly payments by $13.25.

In checking the possibilities, you should subtract from the potential savings any costs involved in making the change. These possible expenses include appraisal and loan fees, title-insurance costs and any penalty that may be provided for in your present mortgage. With the help of your bank or other source of mortgage money, you can quickly discover whether a change is worthwhile—or may be in the future.

If it is, you will have the pleasant choice of taking your profit in either of two forms or a combination of them: you will be able to reduce your monthly

A review and renewal of a mortgage taken out
when money was tight will perhaps lead to
a good deal if money has loosened meanwhile.

payments and still retire the mortgage on the expected date; or you will be able to pay off the mortgage far sooner than anticipated, without any change
in the monthly cost to you.

The examples that follow will help you determine
the wisest and most economical tactics to follow in
various mortgage-handling situations.

Example 1. Payments on your 7-year-old mortgage
now run $183 a month. That amount eats up so much
of your take-home pay that you're forced to let the
regular maintenance slide. The house is getting run-
down. How can you have your payments lowered?

You may be able to reamortize your present mortgage to run for a longer period with lower payments. Arrangements of this sort are ordinarily not popular with lending agencies. But you have an unusually good case: a change that will keep your home properly maintained also offers protection for both you and the lender.

If your present mortgage carries a lower interest rate than those being written today, you will find it more difficult to reamortize. If your rate is much higher than the current one, you might consider obtaining a brand-new mortgage—at today's rate.

The advantage of reamortizing (if your lender will agree to it) is its simplicity. You avoid new loan fees and new title insurance costs. Your total interest cost will be greater, of course, but only to the extent that the repayment period is extended.

Example 2. Your lending agency is not willing to extend the payment time on your mortgage. You are sure you'll have trouble meeting the payments in the years ahead. Is there anything you can do?

You may be able to refinance. This means getting an entirely new mortgage, either from the same lender or another one.

Example 3. You are paying mortgage interest of 8½%. A neighbor tells you he has a 7½% mortgage;

he says this is now a common rate in your locality. Will it pay you to refinance if you can get this rate?

Since the difference of 1 percentage point is large enough to offer you a useful saving, it is a question of balancing the new closing costs you will incur against what you will save in interest. Typically, closing costs run to several hundred dollars. However, by watching certain details you may be able to reduce them substantially.

The largest cost often is for new title insurance. Your policy may be one of those that permit "reissue" title insurance when the old policy has run less than 10 years. This can save you as much as half, but you may not get this reduction unless you ask. This possible saving is a good reason to begin by consulting the same title company that issued the original policy.

Your new property survey may cost $50 or more. This too can sometimes be cut about in half—if you have the same surveyor and he simply gives you a recheck.

Sometimes there is also a loan fee, which may include the cost of appraisal. There will also be legal fees and taxes.

Example 4. How can you tell if refinancing will save you money?

Find out all the new closing costs. Add on any prepayment penalty provided in your present mortgage. Add this total to the amount you now owe. Then find out what the new payments would be for a lower-interest mortgage scheduled to run to the same date as your present one. Here is the way to work this out:

Your 8½% mortgage for $15,000 requires an amortization (principal and interest) payment of $130.17 a month. It is a 20-year mortgage now 5 years old, and your balance is $13,215.

You find you can refinance at 7½%. Total closing costs to you turn out to be $285. To include this, your new mortgage must be $13,500. The amortization table shows that to pay it off in 15 years, the monthly cost will be $125.15.

Thus you will save $5.02 each month for 15 years, but note the warning about a possible disadvantage given in the next example. In the case we're considering, you won't actually begin to be money ahead until some time during the third year after refinancing.

Example 5. You can refinance your mortgage at a lower rate of interest. The difference is enough to pay the new closing costs and still reduce your monthly payment slightly. Are there any other advantages to refinancing? Or any disadvantages?

There is one bonus to refinancing. Besides lowering the interest, you may be able to arrange more favorable terms while you're about it. For instance, you might arrange to cut your monthly payments even more by extending the life of the loan—if this is desirable because of changes in your financial situation. Or you may be able to get an open-end provision, which is handy if you might need money later on to improve your home.

The major disadvantage of refinancing is that the new closing costs added to your mortgage will increase its face amount. You will owe more after refinancing than before, even though the new interest rate will permit either lower or fewer payments to retire the loan.

If you should happen to sell the house within a few years, you'll lose unless you can convince the buyer that the lower rate makes it worth the added price— which it is only if he wants your mortgage.

Example 6. Although your mortgage bears 8% interest, you can't save enough by refinancing to make it worthwhile. Is there any other way you can save on interest?

Within the limits allowed by the terms of your mortgage, by all means prepay it as fast as you can afford to. Prepayment—making extra payments beyond those required by your lender—is equivalent to investing money safely at 8%, an opportunity not easily come by. The return on your investment will then take the form of an increased equity in your home and a mortgage retired sooner.

Example 7. How should you go about making prepayments? Will they protect you later on if you are unable to meet one or more regular payments?

Read your mortgage and consult the lender about the proper method for prepaying. You may be able to pay extra monthly payments— or perhaps only the principal. Sometimes you are required to give written notice 30 days ahead of time.

If your prepayments are of principal only, the lender may agree that these can be credited to any later principal payments that you are unable to make. This can help in an emergency, so try to make such an arrangement.

Example 8. You didn't have much cash to put up when you bought your house. So in addition to a 6¾% first mortgage on it, you have a second mortgage bearing interest at 9%. You can carry the payments easily enough, but you have been shocked at the realization of how much you'll be throwing away on interest over the years. How can you reduce this?

What to do with a second mortgage

High-interest "seconds" are a common problem in some areas, particularly the West Coast. You'd be smart to pay off the second mortgage as fast as your income reasonably permits. First consult the lender about amounts, dates, possible penalties for excessively fast pay-off, and whether he requires advance notice. If you have a source, such as a credit union, or possibly your bank, where you can now borrow at more moderate interest, you may even find it profitable to get money this way to clean up a high-interest second mortgage quickly.

Example 9. You are carrying first and second mortgages, both at 6¾%. Just lately you've accumulated some extra cash; should you invest it or use the money to pay off one of the mortgages?

A second mortgage at such moderate interest was probably made available to you as an incentive to buy the house. Its value on the open market would

be much less than the amount you owe, so you may be able to pay off the mortgage holder for much less than the face value, thus saving on principal as well as interest. You'd find it very difficult to discover any safe investment that would pay you nearly so well.

Example 10. You've been paying on first and second mortgages several years, and improving your home at the same time. When the second mortgage runs out next year, you must make a final payment of $1,000 on it. What arrangements can you make to meet this?

All your payments, plus the improvements, should have built up your equity quite substantially. You may

The dollar appetite of a second mortgage
often makes it hard to take care of a first.

be able to get a new mortgage loan that will: (1) replace the present first mortgage; (2) cover the "balloon" payment of $1,000; and (3) take care of the new closing costs that come with refinancing.

If the interest rate available to you now is lower than that of the existing first mortgage, the difference may pay your extra costs in the long run. If refinancing means a higher interest rate, however, you should first make every effort to find another source for the money you need.

If you are able to make whole monthly payments in advance, you can try to get a similar agreement. Then each of these can take the place of any later full payment that you are unable to make.

Example 11. You have a 5¾% mortgage. Should you make extra payments on it when you have the money to spare?

Many existing mortgages were written years ago when interest rates were much lower than they are now. Prepaying on one of these is a good use of your money, of course, but it may not be the best use.

Placing your extra money elsewhere—in an insured savings account, for instance—may give you about the same return. And you will still have the money available for other purposes if you should happen to need it.

When will you want to sell?

Consider also whether you are likely to want to sell your house during the life of the mortgage. An existing loan at low interest can be an asset in making a sale. The buyer couldn't come close to duplicating it today.

Example 12. Your mortgage payments aren't any particular problem to you now, but you see a crisis ahead. It will strike during the 5 final years of the mortgage when you'll probably have two children in college at the same time. Is there anything you can do to prepare for this?

Regular prepayments on your mortgage, beginning immediately, would be a good solution if the interest rate is higher than you can get for deposits in a savings and loan account. You may find it feasible to retire the mortgage completely before the critical years come, preferably working out a systematic schedule with the lender right away.

Prepayment is also a good solution for people whose retirement, with its income reduction, is not

far away. Given the right prepayment schedule, the mortgage and the homeowner are retired simultaneously.

Example 13. You're falling behind on your mortgage payments. It's a good house, worth more than you owe on it and you want to keep it. What can you do?

Talk to your lender. He should be glad to help you work out a schedule for getting the payments up-to-date. (He doesn't want a foreclosure on your home any more than you do.)

Normally by the time a payment is 10 days overdue, you'll be asked how come. On mortgages insured by FHA or VA, the lender is expected to help you work out a plan to catch up. He may wait almost a year under FHA rules before foreclosing, but he's likely to act sooner if the house is not being kept up. VA allows a mortgage holder 3 months before giving official notice of intention to foreclose in 30 days.

CHAPTER X

Property
Tax
Strategy

Four important things to know about your home and your taxes are:

1. How to tell if the property tax you pay is too much and what to do about it.

2. How to get the maximum income-tax saving from deductible costs of home ownership.

3. How to estimate the effect of these deductions on your income tax in order to determine whether to rent or buy—and what price you can afford to pay.

4. How to minimize or postpone income tax when you sell your home.

Let's take these 5 strategy problems in order.

You may have friends and neighbors with houses comparable to yours who are willing to discuss their tax bills. A quick comparison may indicate that you are right in suspecting the assessed valuation that has been placed on your house is out of line. This can easily happen through a slip or misjudgment on the part of the assessor's office; appraising property is far from an exact science. If you seem to have a case worth pursuing, consult tax records at your city hall or court house, where they are open to the public. This is where you get a precise comparison on as large a scale as you wish.

Property taxes are usually levied in proportion to estimated market value, often of land and "improvements" separately. Then this full value or some fixed fraction of it becomes the "assessed valuation." The annual property tax you pay will be some percentage of this, often expressed in such form as "$9.54 per $100."

You may have to appeal formally to get a reduction in the valuation on which your tax is based or you may get results by informal appeal. Over the years as a homeowner, I have followed the latter course four times—and four times had my taxes reduced. Since my complaints were both legitimate and typical of those of many householders, you may find some suggestive value in the details.

In a rural area 25 years ago I built my first house, using methods often simpler than those in general

use then. My framing of 2x4s spaced 24" and masonry of hollow blocks not plastered or stuccoed on either side—both commonplace today—were radical and economical short-cuts at the time. Having produced a house at far less than normal cost of materials, I was flattered but not particularly pleased to find it valued by the tax people at the same level as more elaborate houses in the area.

I addressed a mild note of protest to the office of the county assessor. One of his assistants turned up a few days later, examined my case and my house, and ruled that my structure should be reclassified—not at all flatteringly this time—as "partially substandard." This cut my tax bill by about 10%.

My second brush with tax people came after a move to an area in which taxes are assessed in 3 parts: land, improvement, personal property. I built a rather elaborate large house, received a proportionately heavy tax bill, but found unwarranted only the high tax on the personal-property part. The $900 valuation, implying at that time nearly $5,000 market value, didn't square with our homemade and makeshift furniture (all we owned and all we wanted in this house, loaded with built-ins that I'd made, wouldn't have fetched $500 at auction) or clothing (no diamonds, no minks, no heirlooms).

The grand piano that wasn't

I asked how come, and the county sent a man to explain the assessment. "To save time we assess personal property in proportion to house value," he explained. "That way we don't have to poke through your closets and everything. A house as big as this, we figure you'd have maybe a grand piano and other expensive things like that. Or you're going to get one."

"Well, I don't," I said. "And I'm not. And so I shouldn't pay tax on something I don't own."

The man eventually agreed there was nothing in the law to justify taxing expectations or even probabilities. When I received my final tax bill, the $900 was crossed out and $300 written in—still an ample figure for our very modest possessions.

A little later when we built another house, a similar informal protest brought agreement that full valuation was premature on an unfinished structure, even though occupied. (Occupancy before completion is permitted in our town, which is small and still comparatively friendly and uninvolved in red tape.) This saved us a useful amount of money that year and some the next.

A foundation without value

My companion argument, that our lot should be valued at less than its neighbors because an extreme slope added to foundation cost, fared less well.

"Right you are," said the assessor's assistant, "So we didn't charge you for the value of the foundation in valuing the structure."

He had me there.

Two years ago the assessment and taxes nearly doubled in a single year on 5 rocky, waterless, unimproved acres we own in northern California. To buttress our argument that the new valuation was improper, we put the land up for sale at the county's figure, listing it with a large real-estate office.

It failed to sell, or even bring an offer, and we used this fact in our letter to complain. The only reply was a form acknowledgment, but the next tax bills showed a drop in "full value" from $15,000 to a more reasonable $10,000. This may be a little high yet, but not so much so as to warrant filing formal objections and attending a hearing many miles from my home.

To me these experiences say that where there is an avenue for informal request for consideration it may be used to save a substantial amount—if your ground for complaint is solid. Avoid formal protest if possible.

Hear what happened to my dentist. He told me about it over the whirr of the drill. "I demanded a hearing on my tax bill," he said. "The county went over all the figures and *jumped* the taxes nearly $100 a year. And there's nothing I can do about it."

My dentist can find solace in the fact that everything he spends for property taxes and interest payments on his mortgage or other indebtedness is fully deductible for income-tax purposes. It is largely because of this that owning a home is usually more economical in the long run than renting a comparable dwelling.

And even in the short run, you may be out-of-pocket fewer dollars each year from the very beginning if you buy rather than rent. Just how this will work out for you depends, first of all, on whether you now itemize deductions when making income-tax returns.

To see how this works, consider the case of Frank B. and Evelyn H. Dempsey. They have two dependents and an income of $17,065. They rent and are contemplating buying. Their exemptions for themselves and the two dependents, at $750 for each, come to $3,000. Their itemized deductions come to $2,108 (mostly for medical expenses and contributions to church and charities). These two amounts subtracted from $17,065 give them a taxable income of $11,957.

The home they have in mind will require a $36,000 mortgage, which they find is available to them for 25 years at 7½% interest. Multiplying the amount of the loan by the interest rate tells them that their first-year interest will total about $2,700. The Dempseys can easily learn what taxes are on the property. It is commonly found on a real-estate listing or can be

learned from the owner's last bill. It is also on public record at the taxing agency. In this instance they learn that last year the taxes were $1,109. Frank adds interest and taxes together to obtain, in round numbers, his potential new deductions of $3,800.

A look at last year's income-tax booklet tells him that for married persons filing joint returns, taxable income between $8,000 and $12,000 is taxed at 22%. Since their taxable income last year, which they can assume is typical of the years just ahead, was $11,957, they can see that the top $3,957 (the amount in excess of $8,000) was taxed at 22%.

This, then, is the percentage they would stand to save by acquiring those new deductions of $3,800, since of course they come off the top. Their net saving on taxes the first year will be 22% of $3,800, or $836: about $70 a month.

The two houses in question are so similar in size, construction, and location that utility and transportation costs will not differ much. If any utility costs—such as heat or water or garbage collections—were paid by the landlord for the rented house, these would have to be subtracted from the rent (or added to the cost of ownership) in making a comparison.

So Frank estimates his monthly ownership costs in the first years will consist of: payments, $266 (taken directly from the payments table); taxes, $92; insurance and maintenance and repair, $50 (Frank is pretty good around the house and does most of the maintenance himself, even as a renter); $30 monthly loss of interest at 6% on $6,000, which Frank will take out of a certificate-of-deposit account and use for down payment, closing costs, and moving-in costs.

The cost of being an owner

The total of all these is $438, which is substantially more than the $375 rent that the Dempseys have been paying, although they have been notified that this is scheduled to go up to $400 when the lease runs out soon.

But when Frank subtracts the potential income-tax saving of $70 from the $438 he will have to put out each month on the average, he finds he can be an owner for $368: $7 a month below his present rental arrangement, $32 a month below next year's rent.

As you apply similar calculations to your own situation, there is one more thing to take into account. If you are now taking the standard deduction on your federal income tax instead of itemizing, your saving will be reduced.

You will find your annual tax saving by adding together the amounts to be paid for interest and property taxes, just as Frank did. But then you should add to these your other possible deductions (medical costs, casualty losses, contributions, possible gasoline and sales taxes, etc.) and subtract the standard deduction to which you would otherwise be entitled.

Certain tax deductions that come with homeownership
often make buying a house a better deal than renting.

Still another special tax advantage* was invented for the benefit of homeowners a few years ago. This is a provision that when you sell your home in order to buy or build a new one, you need not pay income tax on the profits. If you sell your home for a profit, and do not buy another, you are obliged to pay income tax on that profit. If you lose money on the sale of your home, you are not permitted to "take a loss" for income-tax savings.

This is pretty unfair on the face of it, but there are several provisions in the law that you can use to soften the situation. To begin with, if you are faced with a loss on the sale of your residence, you can create a tax saving if you are able to convert that house into a business property. One way to do this is to prove that it was purchased and held in the hope of profit rather than to live in. This is difficult to do if you have failed to make a profit and have been living in the house, unless you can demonstrate that you lived in it for some business reason such as to protect it or make it easier to sell.

It is much more likely that you can make your loss a deductible one by converting the house into a rental property before selling it. Generally speaking, to do this you will actually have to rent it out, not merely offer it for rent. And you'll have to do this for a reasonable length of time, not merely while you are off on a vaca-

* Snidely called a "loophole" when it benefits only other people.

tion or two. Also, your argument will be more convincing if you collect a fair and profitable rent rather than some token sum.

If, as is more likely, you are selling at a profit, there are three income-tax provisions working in your favor.

The profit is taxed as a capital gain if you have had the house for 6 months or more. This means you must count only half the amount of gain. To figure your

A loss incurred in the purchase and sale of a house does you no good on taxes: it's non-deductible.

gain subtract from the selling price selling costs, such as advertising or commission. To the price you paid when you bought it add anything you have spent since to improve it, but not the cost of maintenance and repairs except for fix-up done within the last 3 months before the sale. Then subtract the second total from the first.

You must include half of this amount in your taxable income. Whether you will actually pay tax on it the following April will depend upon whether you use the profit to buy or build a new home. Indeed, some or all of it can be tax-free forever.

Let us see how the tax laws worked out for the J. J. Warrens over a period of many years.

John and Viola bought their first home right after World War II. It cost them $12,000. Seven years later, with two young children squeezing them for space, they added a ground-floor family room. Cost: $3,500.

The following year they sold their house for $23,500. To discover their tax situation, John figured the "basis" of their house: original cost plus improvements, or $15,500. He also calculated the adjusted sales price: actual selling price of $23,500 less 6% real-estate commission ($1,410). Subtracting the $15,500 basis from this figure of $22,090 told the Warrens that their capital gain was $6,590.

Instead of paying income tax on half this amount, the Warrens put all the proceeds of the sale into purchase of a larger house within a year. Thus they postponed their tax liability on that $6,590 capital gain.

If they had built instead of buying, the same rule would apply if they moved in within 18 months.

The postponed tax

For their new house they paid $24,000. Upon preparing to sell it some years later, however, they discovered its cost basis to be only $17,410. The rule is that when you postpone the tax on the sale of your residence you must, in figuring its basis, subtract the amount of the gain from the price of the new house. (The idea is that eventually you will have to pay the tax on this amount.)

So the Warrens were required to subtract the amount of their previous untaxed gain ($6,590) from the actual purchase price of their $24,000 house to get the basis amount: $17,410.

As it happened, the sale John and Vi had in mind fell through, and they decided to rent their house instead. The occasion was a long-awaited year-long world tour.

They were required to report the rent they received as income for tax purposes. On the same form they found space to enter some figures that reduced this amount—and hence the tax on it—considerably. One was all costs of advertising and commissions in connection with the renting; and another was maintenance and repairs during the rental year.

Even more important was depreciation. To figure this they first had to establish a value basis for this purpose, either the original cost or the market value at the time, whichever was lower. Since real estate has been appreciating, they took the original purchase price, $24,000 and estimated that the land (not depreciable) made up $4,000 of this. Of the many methods of depreciation available (a large and highly technical subject) they chose one that allowed 2% a year. So they were able to deduct 2% of $20,000 in addition to the costs mentioned above.

This depreciation of $400 would also have to be subtracted from their basis figure in case of later sale. The basis of the Warrens' $24,000 house had now become $17,010, although the house itself was now worth very nearly $30,000.

"Shall we sell it and pay tax on nearly $13,000?"

That's what the Warrens asked themselves upon their return home. Then they discovered that there are three ways you can permanently avoid paying part or all of this capital gains tax.

How not to avoid taxes

One is by dying. The tax will not be levied against your estate or upon your heirs. Not the best one from your viewpoint, however.

Another is by waiting to make your final house sale until after you have retired. Your taxable income may be so small then that much of the gain will be exempt, especially if you spread the income from the sale over several years.

The third is to make use of a comparatively new tax provision instituted primarily for the benefit of retired people who wish to give up being homeowners and live in a rented home instead.

The third looked best to the Warrens. They wanted to shuck household responsibilities, now that they had had a big taste of the pleasures of travel. Their taxable income from investments was still large enough to make the second possibility unprofitable.

They decided to sell their house only after John reached 65 and to make sure meanwhile that they met one special requirement: occupancy of their home for at least 5 of the 8 years preceding its sale. A year during which they were away would probably not count as occupancy under this rule, but vacations of several months probably would, even though the house were rented out in their absence.

So when John or Vi reaches 65, they can sell their house for, say, $30,000. Taking off nearly $2,000 for selling costs and subtracting the $17,010 basis from the sales proceeds of $28,000, they would show a gain of around $11,000.

For one sale—and only one—in these circumstances (at least one of the couple over 65; principal home, with occupancy during 5 of the last 8 years) all the profit is excludable from taxable income if selling price is $20,000 or less. If more, it is excludable in the proportion that $20,000 bears to the total adjusted sales price.

That $20,000 being about two-thirds of the expected selling price of the Warrens' home, two-thirds of their gain will be tax-free. Forever.

CHAPTER XI

The Canny Renter

Successful, economical renting requires forethought and an organized plan just as surely as buying a home does. Such a plan has six major elements.

1. Although as a renter you are not stuck with your choice, except for the term of your lease, don't be too ready to move frequently. The cost of moving plus the cost of buying draperies, carpets, and extra furniture to fit each new place can be a periodic economic disaster. Hasty moves result in distress sales and big losses on items that won't fit the new house. The saying is: "three moves equal a fire."

2. Try to find housing that includes easy low-cost transportation to your job, or to at least one job if

there are two or more in the family. The lowest rent is not the cheapest if getting to work, schools, shopping facilities, or recreation demands ownership and upkeep of an additional car.

3. Rent with an open mind: a house may not be your best bet. Look all the possibilities over —garden apartment, mobile home park, condominium. Just because your last home was a large house doesn't mean you might not be happier personally and economically in an efficient condominium—or even a houseboat, as families near lakes, canals and rivers are finding out.

4. The amount of rent you pay in dollars and cents can be a deceptive figure. What is included? Some landlords provide free garbage collection, water, TV cable, heat, and gardening. Find out what your rent money is buying before you say, "I'll take it." If the landlord is eager to close the deal he may add a few extras.

5. Do you have to sign a lease? The standard rental lease (provided by a real-estate agent or sold in a stationery store) protects the landlord more than it does you. If you try to move out before the end of the lease, you may be sued for the full amount of rent due for the period stated in the lease. If you pay first and last month's rent, when you move in, as most

Remember that a second car drinks gas the way
any car does, and figure that into the cost
of your housing, if necessary.

landlords now expect, you will lose that last month's
rent, if you move out early, even if the landlord is
willing to release you from the remainder of the lease
period. If you make a cash deposit (often $100 or
more) at the time you move in, what does it cover?
Will it be returned to you when you move out, if you
leave the place in the condition in which you found
it? Or is the deposit actually a cleaning fee which the
landlord will keep no matter how tidy you prove to
be? In some areas the landlord is required to pay interest on any of your monies he holds. Is that the case
in your locality?

Landlords and tenants invariably disagree on the meaning of "clean." Look the place over with the landlord when you move in, point out any deficiencies in cleanliness and any damage to walls, floors, furnishings. Make a written notation of significant damage, have the landlord initial the statement, and clip it to your lease. Written evidence may help get your cash deposit back when the landlord has long ago forgotten that dirt and damage existed when you moved in.

As a renter you should not sign a lease until you have a firm agreement with the landlord on exactly what services he will provide.

Don't rely on a promise that the landlord will fix a leaking sink or replace the non-working oven. Get it in writing. If you agree to make such repairs yourself in return for reduced rent, or if the landlord pays for materials, get that in writing too.

Currently there is a trend toward formation of tenants' associations. One thing they do is promote the drafting of leases that give the tenant a better deal. An American Bar Foundation research project has been drawing up a model lease it hopes will replace the pro-landlord form. You should ask, when signing a lease, for such proposed provisions as these: landlord will keep exterior of dwelling in repair, take care of plumbing defects, see that hot water supply and heat are adequate. In return you can agree to keep your own premises clean, remove trash and garbage, avoid waste, and use fixtures properly. Inquire of your Better Business Bureau or Chamber of Commerce whether you can join a tenants' organization in your locality.

6. As a renter you need to have your belongings protected by insurance. The landlord carries fire, theft, and liability insurance but that does not mean that your possessions or your liability will be covered. You can now get a renter's package insurance policy that is similar to a homeowner's policy. Called

a residence-contents broad form, or tenant form, it covers your personal property and your liability.

With such a policy you'll avoid the expensive woe of Chris Felsen, a medical student, and his wife, who thought their landlord's insurance covered their possessions too. They stored a valuable collection of medical reference books in a warm, dry workshop in the home they rented. Unfortunately the workshop was directly below a bathroom, and a stopped-up toilet inundated ceiling, walls, and floor of the workshop and ruined the books. The landlord's insurance company reimbursed him fully for damage to the

Make a written record of defects in your rented apartment or house so you will not be charged for repairs when you move out.

house, but the Felsens lost a library and there was no insurance to replace it.

7. This accident points to another maxim in dollar-wise renting; know the mechanics of the house you live in. If the Felsens had turned off the water-supply faucet at the base of the toilet as soon as water started running over, instead of waiting for the land-lord to come many hours later, the disaster would have been no more than a minor inconvenience.

Learn the location and operation of utility shut-offs and switch boxes. Ask the landlord for in-structions plus a list of qualified repair shops to call should an emergency arise. You are liable, even in the absence of a specific agreement, to keep the premises in good condition, reason-able wear and tear excepted. Damages caused by your negligence or intentional misconduct could cost you many dollars in court.

How about "free" rent? There are several methods of substituting your own services for part or all of the cash required for rent each month. If you feel able to afford effort more than money, consider the possi-bility of finding an arrangement of this kind.

Such housing is free, of course, only in the sense that you offer services to the landlord instead of cash. So realism requires that before you accept such an arrangement you know how many hours you'll have to put in. Divide that number into the value of the housing you're getting to find out how much per hour your efforts will be producing. Note one nice thing: at least part of this can be tax-free income.

House-sitting, if you can get it, is one of the best of the free-rent deals. Winter and summer there are thousands of people who go off on extended vacations, or seek out better climates for health reasons. They neither need nor want to rent out their permanent homes, but they want them occupied and protected against weather and intruders. They may have

A landlord's insurance doesn't cover your personal belongings as a renter, so take out your own insurance on valuables.

pets that remain behind and need feeding, walking and love. They may have valuable furniture, rare plants, perfect lawns.

Once you establish yourself as an honest, reliable house-sitter in an area where there are many travelers (usually retired or wealthy home owners) you may easily be able to line up enough jobs to keep you permanently housed free at a part-time profession.

That's what Margaret M. Damp does. She writes, in *Harvest Years*, that she and her husband have been getting free rent for the last 6 years and now get more job offers than they can accept. From November to May they have either of these arrangements:

1. Owner pays all expenses, including utilities. The Damps pay a small rent.
2. The Damps pay for heat and utilities, and the rest is free.

Mrs. Damp says her secret of getting repeat house-sitting jobs and good references is to leave the house exactly as she finds it, down to the position of the last towel and shade. She charts the general condition and location of all items during the first hour she's in the house and sees to it that this arrangement is restored exactly before the owners return. The house gives no evidence of the sitters' occupancy.

Since house-sitting of this type requires living in a cold climate while the older owners are in a warm one, the house-sitters can then spend their summers in the opposite climate, if they wish, tending to winter homes and cabins that ordinarily remain vacant during the summer.

House-sitting naturally requires that you have few possessions of your own; that you have some type of income, job, pension that can move with you; and that you will accept frequent moves.

How can you find house-sitting jobs? Consult employment agencies, newspaper ads, bulletin boards

Become a house-sitter and save on housing costs.

in retirement housing areas. Advertise for a sitting job. Check college and university housing offices and bulletin boards. Teachers going on sabbaticals are a source of house-sitting that may last as long as a year.

As caretaker or maintenance superintendent of an apartment or housing complex, you may earn part or full rent, possibly plus some salary. Frequently the landlord wants a husband-wife combination: the husband is employed and the wife can handle routine inquiries, show vacancies, collect rents during the day. The husband takes care of repairs and mechanical problems evenings and weekends.

Get, *in writing*, the exact nature of your duties. Does the gardening, landscaping, pool-maintenance become your job or will it be farmed out? Are you expected to do any redecorating? If you handle rent collections and show vacancies, will you be paid extra for this? Usually a landlord with large apartment houses and frequent vacancies throws in a bonus of 25% to 50% of the first month's rent to the caretaker who gets him a renter for the vacant unit.

Look for hidden drawbacks. Will you and your possessions be fully insured? Is your caretaker's apartment the equivalent of other units in the building, or is it in the basement, loft, or on a noisy street front? Will there be a relief assistant so you get a weekend or evening off? Will you be on duty all night long, in case someone needs a light bulb or just wants to complain?

You can also find places that need redecorating or complete remodeling that may be yours rentfree in exchange for your labor. But be wary lest you overestimate your skills. Unless you have had experience as a carpenter or plumber, it's best to limit yourself to free or low rental deals in which the work consists of comparatively unskilled tasks—yard cleanup, trashhauling, straightforward painting, scrub-up jobs. Get an agreement in writing as to exactly what you are to do, how you are to do it, and what you are to get in return.

Furthermore, a remodeled, cleaned-up, shining place that you've put a lot of labor into may be so attractive that the landlord will soon decide it's time to sell or ask for a higher rent. That's why an arrangement giving you first chance to buy or rent the fixed-up house at an agreed price is best.

CHAPTER XII

The Ultimate: Do It Yourself

If you decide to take a giant step and build your own house with your own hands, you will be plunging into a great adventure. Happily, it is one that can be shared by all members of the family.

You'll come out of this venture with a substantial collection of skills you had never expected to acquire —to say nothing of calluses on both hands. You'll have gained a new and gratifying confidence in your ability to cope. You'll have found the special satisfaction that comes from living day by day in a house that is truly your own creation.

158

And the effect on your economic security will be the most surprising and gratifying of all.

Having gone this route three times myself, I speak from experience. Lest you doubt that the experience has been a happy one, let me add that I've just acquired the lot on which my fourth full-scale house promises to be well along by the time these words are in type.

Who can do it? I know of a couple of women office workers who did it, and also of at least one lone woman, an elderly widow. A young man in Carroll, Iowa, built a home for his wife and baby. He's just an ordinary guy except for having a Medal of Honor and two artificial legs.

Like others who have built for themselves, you will acquire most of the information you need as you go along. Even experienced builders have to do that each time they tackle new methods or new materials. Possibly the most useful source of information is books, beginning with this one. For others, consult your public library, look over the offerings in any large book store, write to the Government Printing Office in Washington, D.C., for a list of booklets on building.

Manufacturers' manuals and booklets are equally important sources. Find them at the lumber yard and in offers in magazine advertisements. They cost little, often nothing. Many magazines are repositories of building lore.

A do-it-yourself house-building project
should begin with homework done in books if
this is your first venture as amateur builder.

A surprising number of people have asked me if I don't have trouble with unions when I do my own work. My answer is that I never have and I've never heard of a do-it-yourselfer who was bothered either by union officers or contractors' associations. There may be parts of the country where things are different.

Codes are both a nuisance and a protection to the amateur builder. He must observe all code requirements, naturally, beginning with the one that says he must start by filing plans and getting a building permit. These can be highly detailed plans, as produced by an architect or a plan service, but they need not be. As for building inspectors, I've heard horror stories from contractors but in my dealings so far with five different inspectors every one of them has been totally helpful. In fact, they're an important addition to the list of sources of information and advice on construction problems. Their code books often tell you such things as what size rafter or joist you need for a given span and condition.

I do my own designing, for better or worse, because that's half the fun. And that way I've never had to learn how to read a blueprint. But it would be folly to put all the work and money that a house involves into a bad plan. So I think that anyone who draws his own should at least have a good architect go over it unless he has reason to believe he's done a good job.

As for financing, the house you build yourself is better-than-ordinary security because you know so much of what you are putting into it is effort instead of just dollars. But because it is not the routine situation that the money people are used to, the owner-built house is most difficult to finance. In my experience, however, when you have your lot paid for, that gives you security for a building loan. This will ordinarily be set up so that you can draw specified amounts as you complete each step in the project. Your increased equity as you complete portions of the house gives security for more of the loan. When the house is complete you convert the building loan to a regular mortgage, which will come to only a small fraction of the value of the house.

We paid for our first house by purchasing a building lot from savings, then paying for building materials out of income. Though it meant living crudely for a while, we were thus able to pay all building costs with money that otherwise would have gone for rent.

Proceeds from eventual sale of the first house more than paid for a more costly site and materials for a

As your construction proceeds, proceeds of a building loan will be made available in installments.

second, larger house. When the building urge struck again, several years later, we had no difficulty getting a mortgage on it for enough to buy a choice lot, build our present house, and supplement our income while we built.

I was pleased to learn on that occasion that the house and lot in which we had invested less than $20,000 (but a good deal of time and energy, of course) could then be mortgaged for $48,000 if I wanted that much.

How long it takes to build a house is much more variable than the cost. Working part time, averaging several hours a day, I built mine over a period of nearly four years. However, at the end of the first year enough was done so that we could move in.

A smaller, simpler place should go up much faster. My wife and I built our first house 20 years ago—a three-bedroom 1,200-square-footer. On that one we started site preparation in September, and moved in the day before Christmas. Things were pretty primitive, however—many partitions and ceiling still lacking, building paper standing in for some windows, no interior doors.

Time you'll take will depend most particularly on how much help you can commandeer. Actually, a home-building project is always interesting enough to attract volunteer help from friends and neighbors.

Neighbors and others will frequently be glad to lend
hands to an amateur builder for heavy but quick jobs.

Fortunately the really heavy jobs, such as lifting beams
into place, usually take only a few minutes. A hoist
or woodworking clamps judiciously used are often
equal to an extra pair of hands.

So much for generalities. If you're going to think
at all seriously about biting off a whole housebuilding
project for yourself, the section that follows in small
type is for you. If not, jump ahead to where the
larger type begins again.

1. Decide what kind of house you want—not its shape or what it is going
to look like but its size and function. This means you must decide who and
what you are as a family and how you wish to live. Don't draw, or choose,
a plan yet, except to the extent you have to in order to make these decisions.

2. Get your land.

3. Now it is time to arrive at a plan, as discussed a few pages back. You
will also have to choose your construction methods and materials in general
(concrete slab or wood-framed floor; frame or masonry walls) unless your
plan specifies these things.

4. Adapt plan to site. Its slope may affect type of foundation. Its size and shape and existing trees will affect where on the lot your house should go.

5. Get your building permit and find out what codes govern construction in your area. You may have to make some changes in your plans to conform.

6. Consult the proper city authorities and utility companies about water, power, gas, sewer, and telephone service. You'll want to keep requirements in mind from the beginning, and you'll want to get the first two in just as soon as you can.

7. Determine house location precisely by driving stakes at corners, carefully observing required setbacks. Put up batter boards to hold string that will mark house lines after stakes are removed during excavating. (If you lack a book that tells you just how to do this, it is time to augment your library.)

8. Dig, build lumber forms, and pour the concrete footings that will hold up your house. Continue with foundation walls of concrete or block, unless these are integral with your footings.

9. Pour a concrete slab floor; or place sills and joists and install a subfloor of lumber or plywood on these joists.

10. Now you will quite suddenly begin to make visually exciting progress. You'll frame the walls (mostly with 2x4 lumber placed 16" or 24" center to center) and the roof.

11. Before going too far you should get your plumbing roughed in. This means drain lines and vents through the roof and connection to sewer, as well as water supply lines. You'll install fixtures later.

12. You may want to rough in your electric wiring now too. This means putting in a service entrance (the thing the electric company will drop wires to) and running wires to the various boxes that will hold switches and receptacles and the like.

13. Traditionally your wall framing will include diagonal bracing and will require a layer of sheathing (in the form of lumber or plywood or panels of insulation board) on the outside, and probably building paper as well. You may prefer to eliminate these two or three layers by using plywood so that it does four jobs in one step.

14. For the house I am building now I am using a ruggedly handsome new redwood plywood which has shallow grooves cut the length of it at 12-inch intervals to give the effect of reverse board-and-batten siding. It has been treated at the mill to make painting or staining unnecessary—actually saving a fifth step. When this material is nailed according to specifications, it serves all the purposes of bracing, building paper, sheathing, and siding.

15. After siding—or before, if you want quick shelter from the weather, comes roofing. Usually this will be some kind of shingle for a sloping roof or tar-and-gravel for a flat or nearly flat one. The latter type, which involves hot tar and tons of weight, is not something I would even consider tackling.

16. Put in doors and windows. There aren't going to be any real windows, by the way, in my new house. Just fixed glass for view and sunlight, translucent plastic sheets for privacy combined with daylighting, and sliding patio doors that give ventilation as well as access to private decks. But ours is a mild climate.

17. Order makes little difference by now. You can proceed to insulation, partitions, interior wall materials, floor finishing and ceiling. There'll be counters and closets and built-ins to construct, electrical and plumbing fixtures to install, inside and outside trim to complete. Heating may go in at this stage or—depending on the type—much earlier, some of it possibly before you pour concrete.

18. Your fireplace may go in now, too, if it's the modern metal kind. If it's masonry you'll have started its construction earlier but may be completing it now.

19. Decks, porches, and patios are important parts of a smoothly functioning house. Although these may be the final jobs you do, ways to connect them to the house should be allowed for during the main construction.

20. You may prefer to let your driveway wait until a late stage also, to protect it against possible damage by heavy delivery trucks.

Of course you'll make mistakes, a lot of them. I've made more than I can remember, or would want to, but I haven't made any—yet—that I couldn't somehow remedy. Professionally built houses have mistakes in them, too. Often they are permanent ones, because no one is prepared to pay the cost of doing something about them.

But if you're neither careless nor reckless you're not at all likely to make dangerous mistakes— gas pipes that leak, walls that fall down, wires that electrocute. Houses that are built by today's standard methods are overdesigned to include an enormous margin for error. In most areas, codes tell you what to do to be more than safe, and inspectors see that you do it.

The house you build for yourself is likely to be customized far beyond the standards of even good custom construction. You have the chance to make your decisions on details as you go along. The result is that your owner-built house is likely to differ from ordinary houses in having an unusual number of built-in desks, closet drawers, bookcases, specialized storage, couches, and window seats. Such things are brutally expensive when done for you, but building them yourself is cheaper than buying equivalent furniture.

There are many materials and methods that are especially suitable for the owner-builder, just as there are many that are better avoided.

I would say that plaster is a great material to stay away from, and stucco is another. Unless your eye says otherwise, these somewhat difficult materials are less attractive than alternatives you can quickly learn to handle well and comfortably. Although putting on paint is not an especially difficult art, I find it a tedious one. I prefer to avoid materials that require painting if only because of something I discovered long ago: painting leads to repainting too many times over the years. This is one of the reasons I avoid gypsum board, the usual substitute for plaster, and use lumber or plywood paneling instead. Gypsum board is excellent, however, as a backer for plywood where you want to add stiffness and sound deadening; and it makes a simple fire wall where codes require one, as between dwelling and attached garage.

Slate on a concrete slab makes a beautiful bargain floor. Instead of stock windows I make as much use as I can of large, fixed sheets of glass set directly into framing. Sliding glass doors provide most of the needed ventilation.

Expose, don't trowel, your concrete

Concrete work can be organized so that the plywood and lumber for forms can be cleaned up and used for construction. Exposed-aggregate driveways, patios, and walks are easier than troweled ones—and handsomer and safer besides.

Rough tongue-and-groove pine, painted white or off-white and immediately scraped with a broad knife, makes an attractive ceiling. In a warm climate, use the 2" kind and let it also serve as a roof deck.

For easy fireplace construction, take advantage of modern devices. A steel circulator core helps you build a masonry fireplace that won't smoke up the room yet yields far more heat than the ordinary kind. For situations where masonry construction would be difficult, investigate what is called a zero-clearance fireplace unit. This kind is all metal, can be placed almost anywhere—on a wood floor, against a wood wall—yet can be installed so it looks no different from the traditional sort.

Don't be stingy about investing in tools. All that equipment you may have been coveting for years can now be yours without qualms because it will become part of a project that is saving you money at a great rate. Good power tools, especially, will save you months of time and give you precision that most of us will never be craftsmen enough to get with hand tools.

The most important is a solidly anchored saw, preferably the radial-arm type. Next come an electric drill and two portable saws—circular and saber. If you do much with built-ins and furniture you'll soon feel the need of some other common power tools. Most helpful are jointer, band saw, portable belt sander, and a router with a planer attachment.

When a machine does something more easily than you can, let the machine do it. Like mixing cement.

When shopping for tools, remember that you're no longer a mere hobbyist. You're up to serious business and you want tools to match. Buy good, durable stuff of at least semipro caliber, secondhand if necessary. Rent what you can't afford to buy, or need only occasionally.

As a general rule it's simply not sensible to knock yourself out competing with machinery. If you have

a big excavating job that is accessible to powered equipment, let the machine do it. Mixing your own concrete seldom pays. In most areas you can buy the transit-mixed kind and have it dumped where you want it—all for what it would cost you to buy the cement and sand and gravel that it is made of. Except for especially difficult conditions of access, when you mix concrete you are working for nothing.

Which other chores you farm out instead of doing them yourself should depend on the nature of your skills, your willingness to learn, and the precise conditions. One thing very much worth doing yourself is shopping around. On most major purchases I have found about 20% difference between highest and lowest quotations, a saving to be had on several thousand dollars of purchases in the course of building a house.

Since you won't have predetermined specifications to meet, you can grab other bargains: odd lots of lumber, specials on plywood, last year's appliances being closed out. Also, you can take the time to select and cut with care, so can frequently use a cheaper grade of lumber than a contractor could.

To keep costs down on small purchases not worth getting bids on, you may be able to arrange a standing discount at several suppliers. The understanding I have with four lumber dealers and one plumbing-supply house is that I pay normal over-the-counter prices less 10%, but must pay within 10 days after being billed to get this advantage.

This probably sounds remarkable. But, speaking very roughly, the cost of a house these days splits into three equal parts: materials, labor, and contractor's overhead and profit. When your own efforts replace both labor and contractor, you save (or earn!) practically all of the latter two-thirds—except to the extent that you decide to hire certain jobs done for you.

With most of the figures in on a house built by an owner-builder whose affairs I have watched closely, several years ago, I can test that estimate. This house is a big one, with five bedrooms—3,000 square feet including the double garage. Following the usual practice of counting half the garage space, that's 2,800 square feet for $13,966, or almost exactly $5 a square foot. This is for materials alone, except for roofing and rough plumbing, which were contracted. The owner-builder did everything else himself. While two other houses of comparable quality went up in the same block, the contract on each was at about $14 a foot, to which should be added about 10% for miscellaneous and design costs—or something over $15 a square foot.

This house recently sold for $59,900. Since several offers came in at almost that amount, it is fair to take that as true market value. However, about $15,000 of the gain should be attributed to increase from $5,000 to perhaps $20,000 in the value of the land this house sits on. But, even putting that aside as an indirect gain from the building project, this amateur builder earned himself a clean $28,000.

APPENDIX

Model Checklists
to Use in Looking
for a House

1. Location

1. Is there a nearby shopping center, one large enough to offer a variety of stores, including a supermarket, in your price class?

2. How good are the schools? Are they really within walking distance—walk to see—or will you have to transport children daily? Or is there a bus service?

3. Is there public transportation? How costly? How rapid? Does it run on holidays and late in the evening? Could you really walk to and from the bus stop? At night? Don't take anyone's word for this. Make a trial walk.

4. Is the neighborhood relatively safe? What kind of fire and police protection? How close is the nearest fire hydrant? Are there street lights?

5. How convenient is the street? Is it scheduled for widening? (A very wide street encourages fast driving and endangers children as well as producing more noise.) Or is the street a quiet cul-de-sac or dead end? How is parking?

6. Are improvements in: curbs, paving, storm sewer, sidewalk, underground utilities? Or will you be assessed for these later and have to do without them in the meantime?

7. How close are community facilities? Church, park, swimming, golf and tennis facilities, playground, library?

8. Is water supply safe, reliable, soft enough? Is the pressure adequate?

9. Is there TV cable? Will you need a high aerial?

10. Do you have protective zoning and a zoning commission that stands firm? Or may the area gradually change over to semi-commercial, hotel, or industrial use?

11. Are neighboring houses well-kept? Any trash in street or behind houses?

12. What are the neighbors like? Talk to them. Check the area on weekdays as well as weekends. Are there mobs of children playing in the street, a lot of dogs barking, other pets such as an early-morning crowing rooster, a donkey that brays, teenagers with hot rods or motorcycles?

13. What's the local mini-climate like? Are there frequent high winds? Does wind bring smoke or smells from other areas? (Check this during the week when nearby factories, if any, are operating.) Is the house near a swamp, a flood problem-area? Is it in a fog belt or a warm belt?

14. Are there other houses for sale? Find out why. Even if you can get a pretty good deal on price, would you be able to sell again easily without excessive loss?

HIGH WATER
SPRING '67

FALL '68

SUMMER '69

SPRING '71

Conclusion: not a house
you'd want at flood times.

2. The Outside

1. How does the house sit on the lot? Has it been placed to make best use of natural land-scaping, the sun, the wind, the view, the position of neighboring houses, the street?

2. Does the house have pleasing design? Not too many angles and odd changes in level? No awkward roof line and stalky chimney?

3. Was the house designed by an architect? (This can be a clue to good design if you don't trust your own judgment.)

4. Is outside paint or stain in good condition? If recently painted, was preparation adequate—surface scraped to remove blisters and peeling paint or were they painted over?

5. Is driveway approach easy to negotiate? Safe for backing out? Are there hedges or fences that conceal oncoming traffic?

6. Is driveway of good material? If of concrete, are there large cracks, displacement? Is it thick enough to hold the weight of a heavy vehicle? If blacktop, any potholes? Is it pitched for good drainage?

7. Does house appear to sit level and look solid? Any obviously out-of-plumb lines?

8. How many different materials used? More than two usually create a cluttered, cheap look, even though the materials themselves are of good quality.

9. Does house blend with contour and shape of the land?

10. Is house devoid of gimmicks? No useless decorations, false front, gingerbread trim, imitation weather vane or dovecote?

11. Does garage blend with house? (Attached garage is best.)

12. Are garage doors wide enough for easy entrance? Are they automatic? If not, do they open easily? Can they be locked?

13. Is garage light and airy, suitable for workshop or play as well as cars?

14. Is there adequate outdoor lighting, especially on walks and near garage?

15. What is the roof material? Best materials are tile, slate, shakes. Tar-and-gravel roof is good if roof is flat or slightly pitched. Are there any obvious cracks, tears, bare spots? (Check for a leaking roof by visiting the house on a rainy day.)

16. Are there gutters? (Aluminum or plastic best.) Any rust stains from leaking gutters? If no gutters, does rain drip onto prepared gravel area?

17. Are there overhangs where needed to protect you and the house from the weather?

18. Are there outdoor patios protected from wind and placed to trap sunshine?

19. Are there several entrances to the house, including one with easy access from garage to kitchen and basement?

20. Are there vents where needed to give plenty of ventilation to attic as well as to areas below floor level?

21. Are there water connections for hoses on all sides of the house?

22. Are there protected electrical outlets, especially in patio areas?

23. If there is a large lawn and garden, is there a sprinkler system? How many hours of yard work?

24. Is approach to the front door easy and attractive? Is it wide enough for easy access for people and furniture moving?

25. Is there a bell or intercom? Is there a window or peephole in the front door?

3. Entryway

1. Is the access floor made of tile, slate, or other material impervious to stains and water?

2. Is the front door solid-looking, with a good lock and bolt?

3. Is the entrance well-lighted? So you can identify visitors easily, lighting should be stronger outside than in.

4. Is there a closet for guest clothing?

5. Are living areas of the house concealed from entry to give privacy as well as protection?

6. Is there easy access to other parts of the house, especially to kitchen and bedrooms?

4. Kitchen

1. Is this room—the most important room in the house—easily accessible from all other parts?

2. Is it large enough (a minimum of 8 × 12 feet if well arranged)?

3. Is it close to dining room and any outdoor eating areas?

4. Are open distances between appliances and counters at least 4 feet? (Distance from sink to range should be not greater than 6 feet; to refrigerator, no more than 7 feet.)

5. Is there more than one type of counter surface? (Ideal is heatproof ceramic tile near stove and oven, smooth plastic near sink and refrigerator, with sections of wood for chopping and marble for pastry-making.)

6. Are counter widths at least 2 feet?

7. Is counter space arranged so there are areas for placing bundles near entrance, putting items near stove, refrigerator, sink?

8. Is there a variety of cabinet and storage space, such as narrow shelves for spices, shelving for large pans, slots for trays, assorted compartments for a variety of dishes, canned and packaged foods?

9. Is there a pantry?

10. Is there storage space for brooms, mop, newspapers, large equipment?

11. Are there built-ins—a mixer, toaster, warming oven, instant-hot water faucet, garbage grinder, bread slicer?

12. Is there an adequate ventilating fan over the stove? (The kind that vents directly outdoors is best.)

13. Are counters and built-ins the right height for you? If oven is built-in, is door low enough so you won't burn your arm when you reach in?

14. Is there adequate light, both artificial and natural? (A skylight gives good all-over lighting but can let in too much heat in a warm climate, especially if it cannot be opened.)

Conclusion: closet space
for cleaning materials inadequate.

15. Is the floor material durable and easily cleanable? (Cork and carpeting are easier under-foot than the more durable, hard-surface materials such as slate, brick, or tile; pure vinyl comes somewhere between in both respects.)

16. Does kitchen have an eating bar or space for informal family meals?

17. Is there a desk, shelves for cookbooks, enough drawer space?

18. Is there room for expansion? (A too tightly planned kitchen may not permit the acquisition of a larger refrigerator, double oven, or even an additional wastebasket.)

19. What kind of kitchen walls? (They should be easily washable; area behind sink should be a backsplash of something durable like tile or plastic.)

20. What kind of sink? (Stainless steel is more costly, more durable, but shows waterspots. Chip- and stain-resistant enamel is easier to care for, may be damaged if someone drops a heavy pan. Sink should be large, especially if divided. Try putting in a large pan to see if it can be washed easily.)

21. How much cabinet space? (FHA says there should be at least 50 square feet of shelf space in wall and base cabinets combined. Carry a tape measure and check.)

22. Will cabinets be easy to clean? Need frequent repainting?

23. Are there plenty of electrical outlets in counter areas? Is there more than one circuit, so all outlets may be used at once without blowing a fuse?

5. Bathrooms

1. How many? (The more elaborate houses today usually have one master bath, a bath for children's rooms, a powder room for guests, and another half-bath off the family room. But remember that having many bathrooms can mean a lot of cleaning.)

2. Watch out for fixtures, carpets, and walls in luxury materials or dark colors that require constant upkeep. That black, oversize Roman tub will not only show every bit of lint but will require many gallons of hot water to get higher than your ankles.

3. Where are the bathrooms located? Is the bathroom door protected from public view? Do you have to go through someone's bedroom to get to a bathroom? Are fixtures separated? Two lavatories? Toilet partitioned from tub? Is tub long enough, deep enough for a tall person?

4. Do fixtures have brand names? (Cheap fixtures may be made by well-known manufacturers but the name is understandably left off.)

5. What kind of faucets? Look for solid brass with heavy coat of chrome or brushed steel. Mixing faucets are best.

6. What type of toilet? Siphon-jet vortex (best)? Simple wash-down model (worst)? Wall mounted (easiest to clean under)? Is built-in toilet paper holder in a convenient spot? Is room sound-proofed to prevent loss of privacy?

7. Is the shower in a tub or a separate unit at least 36" to 40" square? Does shower nozzle have self-cleaning head with flexible joint? Is the floor of shower slip-proof? What kind of walls? Enameled steel will chip, be cold to touch, make a loud noise if bumped.

8. If shower is in the tub does it have an automatic device to return water flow to tub? Is there a translucent safety glass or plastic door?

9. Is medicine cabinet large enough? Is there an extra cabinet with childproof lock?

10. What kind of floor? (Tile is durable but cold with a breakage hazard. Pure vinyl is good.) If carpet, is it removable for easy washing? Can it be scrubbed if of the permanently installed type?

11. What kind of bathroom lighting? (Fluorescent can be unflattering.) Any area lighting for makeup or shaving? Is there an outlet for a shaver?

12. Is there auxiliary heat (heat lamps near tub and shower or supplementary electric heater)?

13. Is there space for linens, large bathroom accessories such as hamper, scale, bathstool? Plenty of strong towel bars?

14. Are there safety items? Grab bars in tub and shower, shower light protected from water, electric outlets out of reach of tub or shower?

15. Do fixtures have easily accessible shut-off faucets?

16. How soon does the hot water arrive? (Try it.) (If water heater is at a distant point the hot water pipes should be well insulated or on an instant-hot-water circulating device.)

17. What kind of wall materials? Tile still cleans and wears best. Formica, vinyl or similar washable materials are good. If wallpaper, is it scrubbable?

Conclusion: hot water arrival time
leaves something to be desired.

18. Are bathroom washbasins large enough for hairwashing, quick laundry, as well as male splashing? Does basin have cabinet storage space below? Is basin surrounded by an adequate counter?

19. If basin and tub as well as enclosures are of fiberglass, how durable? (Fiberglass is warm, has attractive integral color, is easy to clean but damaged by harsh cleaning materials and abrasives.)

20. Are there adequate built-in mirrors, well-lighted?

21. Adequate window ventilation in bath (window over the tub may be drafty)? Is there a ventilating fan? A fan plus a window that opens is a good combination for removing steam quickly.

22. How small is too small for a bathroom? Do you bump a fixture when you bend over or stretch out your arms? You can't often take a bath in a house you're inspecting but you can always try out the action and practicality of the fixtures. Drop a cigarette or wad of paper into the toilet and watch how efficiently it flushes down.

6. Living Room

1. Is it a welcoming private room with areas for reading, conversation, games, TV-watching? Or is it merely the main road to kitchen and bathrooms?

2. What kind of flooring? (Hardwood is beautiful but noisier and more difficult to care for than carpeting.) If the floor is of wood or tile, will you still need to invest in area rugs?

3. Is there a fireplace? Is it a circulating type that sends warm air into the room? Does it smoke? Look for telltale evidence above the opening. Is there an adequate hearth to protect the floor from sparks? Hearth should be at least 2 feet wide, of slate, stone, or tile.

4. Is there plenty of natural light from windows that look out on a view, rather than into the neighbor's windows or toward the roof? Is the artificial light efficient and attractive? Are there plenty of outlets, several on each wall and one or two in the floor for lamps? There should be an outlet within 6 feet of any point along the walls.

5. Are there built-ins? Bookshelves, cupboards, magazine shelves or racks, window-seat? Look for available space for any needs of your own, a place for a piano, stereo equipment, game table.

6. Is there plenty of wall space for furniture? Room for several groups to use the room at the same time? Space enough for a large party if you're a family that likes lots of guests? Wet bar?

7. What kind of ceiling? Note that an impressive two-story or cathedral ceiling may mean a difficult or expensive room to heat.

8. Does room seem cozy? Any drafts? (Feel around windows and doors for evidence of air leakage.)

9. Does room seem spacious? (Without seeing furniture in it you may not be able to judge. Pace if off or measure with a tape measure; draw a plan and superimpose your own furniture diagrams on it when you get home.)

7. Dining Room

1. Is it separate from the living room? If not, will the open plan fit in with your way of eating and cleaning up?

2. How many steps from dining room to kitchen?

3. How large a table will fit in? (Measure the room and your furniture for fit. A dining chair needs 2 feet on each side and another 2 feet behind it.)

4. Is there a built-in buffet? Shelves or cupboards for china?

5. Is dining room isolated from kitchen clatter and odors? In open planning a well ventilated kitchen with a quiet floor can contribute to dining comfort.

6. What kind of floor? (Scraping chairs are noisy and destructive to many types of flooring.)

7. If floor is carpeted, will carpet stand up to rigorous cleaning of food stains?

8. Bedrooms

1. How many bedrooms does your family need? Is a guest room essential or will a study or family room convert adequately?

2. Is there space for the bed arrangement you have in mind? (Allow at least 102 inches width for twins. Use these figures to check: twin bed is 39 inches by 72 inches; double bed, 54 inches by 72; queen, 60 inches by 72 inches; king, 72 by 72 inches or 72 by 84 inches.)

3. Is space sufficient for any special items such as an extra-long bed for a very tall person, a chaise longue, baby crib?

4. Is there a place for the furniture you now own and wish to retain (dressers, dressing tables, cedar chest, etc.)?

5. Are bedrooms close to bathrooms? Does master bedroom have its own bathroom?

6. Do bedrooms have adequate privacy and soundproofing from the rest of the house? (Thick walls may be little help if doors are flimsy.)

7. What kind of floor covering? (Carpet is most comfortable and quiet but more liable to damage, especially in children's rooms. Carpet is not recommended in the bedroom of an allergy sufferer. Small rugs may lead to falls. Vinyl and cork are easy to clean, resilient, attractive.)

8. Is ventilation adequate? (In most climates there should be cross-ventilation—windows that can be opened on at least two walls of the room.)

9. Is lighting adequate? A reading light over the bed? Automatic lights when you open closet doors? Are there electrical outlets near desk and dressing table?

10. How's the security? (Most important: windows should ventilate without being openable from outside. Combine this feature with a bedroom door that locks and a bedside phone extension or jack and even an intruder who gets into the house will not be in your room before you can summon help.)

11. Most important of all—and now required by many building codes—is there an emergency exit? (Needed is an easily opened window, big and low enough to crawl through quickly and safely.)

9. Closets and Storage

1. How much is enough storage space? (Compare by measuring closets and cabinets in your present house. A closet should be 24 to 30 inches deep; a walk-in closet usually wastes space in the middle. Two medium-sized closets are better than one large one.)

2. Do closets have strong rods at several heights? Shoe racks? Shelves at various heights for hats, bags, accessories?

3. Is there special storage space for out-of-season clothing and blankets? Sports equipment? Possessions that absent members leave behind for safekeeping? A closet for brooms, sweeper? A place for suitcases, trunks? Is there storage space for fireplace wood, preferably near the fireplace?

4. Do closets in bedrooms have sliding doors rather than swing-open doors, which take up room and pose a hazard to mobility?

5. Are there possibilities for adding storage? Is there room in the garage for shelves?

6. Is there a coat closet near the front entrance?

7. Are existing storage spaces too deep and dark? Could they be remodeled easily for efficiency?

10. Utility and Laundry Room

1. Is it convenient to bedrooms, bathrooms, and kitchen (rather than situated in a faraway basement or garage)?

2. Are spaces large enough for your present appliances? Measure!

3. Is the area wired to take a 240-volt dryer? Is there an outdoor vent for the dryer?

4. Is the laundry area adequately ventilated to remove heat and steam?

5. Is there a place for ironing? A built-in ironing board?

6. Are there cupboards and shelves for laundry materials? A counter for folding clothes?

7. Is there an area for mending? A place for a sewing machine?

8. Is there good natural and artificial lighting?

9. Is there a floor drain to take overflow from a misbehaving washer?

10. Is there a utility tub for hand-laundering chores?

11. Staircases and Halls

1. Are stair treads at least 10 inches deep and no more than 8 inches high?

2. Is the staircase wide enough to permit furniture transport?

3. Do all stairways have good safety rails?

4. Does the staircase feel comfortable, easy to use even when your arms are loaded?

5. Does hallway permit easy passage for two people going opposite directions at once?

12. The Mechanical Side

1. Will the house be comfortable in all kinds of weather? (Visit it on a windy day, a rainy day, a sunny day.)

Conclusion: access to
laundry-utility room not easy.

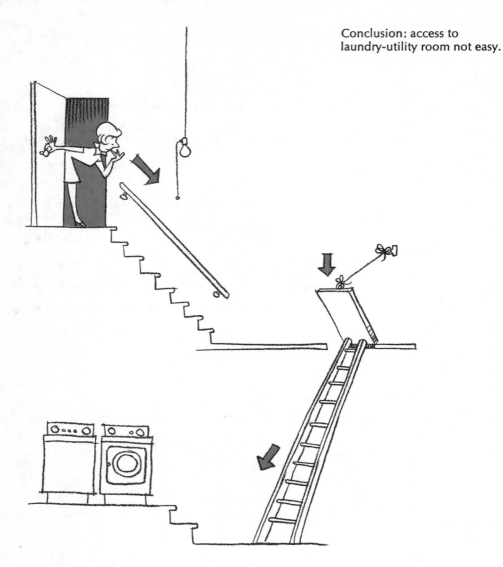

2. Is there insulation? What kind? (Anything less than 3 inches of mineral wool in ceilings and walls is inadequate in most climates.) If there are floors over open or crawl spaces, do they have an inch or more of insulation?

3. What kind of heating? (Ask the real-estate agent or owner to turn it on and off. Listen for annoying sound effects. Ask to see figures on heating costs.) Is there a central air-conditioning system?

4. Are water supply and pressure adequate both inside and outside the house? Do faucets make noise when you turn them on?

5. Do sinks or toilets show rust or green stains, indicating that water is corrosive? How does the water taste? Is water excessively hard? Try making soapsuds. If water is hard, soap will become scummy.

6. You can't look at the wiring in the walls, but how does the electrical-entrance box look? Does it have a modern circuit breaker instead of fuses? Are there markings to tell you which circuits control which rooms? As you walk through the house can you switch lights off and on to create a path of light? Is there any dimming of lights when many fixtures are on or an appliance is plugged in? Are lighting fixtures well designed? Easy to clean? Easy to reach when bulbs must be changed?

7. Is there adequate noise control? (Bedrooms and bathrooms should be separated from other rooms and preferably buffered by halls, closets, bookshelves. An acoustical ceiling helps hush sound within a room. So does a heavy carpet, which also muffles footsteps.)

8. Is there a burglar alarm? Fire alarm? Are doors and windows properly lockable and located for good security and safety?

9. Is the basement finished for family use? If not, are the conditions of headroom, freedom from posts, and humidity such that refinishing would be feasible?

Conclusion: heating system noisy, inefficient; window expensively drafty.

13. New Home List

1. Has the builder done other houses in the area? Are buyers generally satisfied with his work? Does he guarantee his houses? For how long? In writing? Has he willingly honored his guarantee on other houses he's built? Does he live in the development? Is he in the phone book? Does his sales technique stop short of high pressure? (Ask about his reputation at your local Better Business Bureau, your bank, your Chamber of Commerce.)

2. If you're buying from a model, will your house be surrounded by the same features, or will some be extras? Will complete landscaping, as for the model, be included? Or will the "landscaping" you get be grass seed and one tree? Will lot size be the same?

3. If the development is new, are recreation areas, club house, and swimming pool on-paper prospects only? Have they been completed, or is there a fixed completion date?

4. Is the new house on fill? It may settle excessively unless the fill has been in for at least a year before the house is constructed.

5. Does the price of the house include streets, curbs, sidewalks, underground TV cable, underground power lines?

6. Has the builder retained most existing trees and interesting land features such as rocks and shrubs? (Beware of the quickie builder who bulldozes off such assets to speed up his job.)

7. Will the price of your house include screens, storm windows, any of the deluxe decorating features that you saw in the model house—extra-deep carpeting, mirrored closet doors, an intercom system, room divider, etc.?

8. Will your house be air-conditioned? The model house usually is.

9. Will you get your choice of lots? Can you have the lot at the dead end, the one near the creek, the one at the edge of the park? At how much additional cost? (A model house is usually on the choicest lot, the one with the view of a forest or lake or mountain. Sometimes you can make a good buy, when all other houses in the tract are sold, and the model is available with extras but at no extra cost.)

10. Did the builder use a good architect? Or did he pick his plans out of a book? (Some established developers of large tracts pay thousands of dollars for first-rate plans. Details may be worked out far more carefully than would be feasible for a single house of moderate cost.)

11. Will the builder complete your house on time? (Get this in writing. A long delay can cost you money and seriously inconvenience you if you have to sell your present home and move out to an interim location while waiting.)

12. What assurance do you have as to quality of fixtures and appliances? (Quality and cost level can be judged to some extent by looking at the brand names in the model house or, better, as listed in the contract. Ask other homeowners about durability and convenience of fixtures.) Did the builder or manufacturers stand back of guarantees when there were breakdowns?

13. If you ask for changes and extras before construction begins, what will each cost? After the house is started? (Get the details of changes and cost in writing.)

14. Are you allowed any free options in floor plan, in carpets and flooring, in paint colors, in cabinetwork?

House Detective-Kit

1. When you go house-comparing, take along a tape measure—or become a human yardstick by calibrating yourself:

Measure your shoe length—usually about 10 inches for a woman, 12 for a man. Use this information to step off a room or to check size of a floor tile (commonly 6, 9, or 12 inches square) and multiply to find room dimensions.

Measure your normal step. Or learn to pace at average of 3 feet.

You can measure a room in seconds if you know your "wingspread" or outstretched fingertip-to-fingertip span. This will probably be almost exactly your height—another useful figure. Knowing the width of your handspan will be useful in measuring important little distances, such as shelf widths, bookcase widths, and window sizes.

2. Carry a pencil and small notebook. Use them while you're looking. It may not seem so at first, but after you've viewed a dozen assorted dwellings even the important features of the most desirable houses will be a blur in your mind.

3. On a pad of ruled (graph) paper you can rough out a floor plan in jigtime. The kind with 4 lines to the inch is most useful.

Payment Tables

How to use: first turn to the section for the interest rate you will be paying. Find the column headed by the number of years your mortgage is to run. Look down the column to the point opposite the number of dollars of the face value of the mortgage. This will tell you the amount of monthly payments necessary to amortize the mortgage fully (or pay off the contract of sale) so that after the period of years given the house will be yours, free and clear.

If the precise amount of your loan is not in the table, you can quickly calculate it. Like this: Suppose you are borrowing $32,250 at 7½% for 30 years. In the 7½% section of the table, under the heading "30 years," you find the figures for $32,000 ($223.75) and for $200 ($1.40). To the total of these you add half the figure for $100 (half of .70 is .35). Your monthly payments will be $225.50.

Notes

6%

TERM AMOUNT	5 YEARS	10 YEARS	15 YEARS	20 YEARS	25 YEARS	30 YEARS
$ 100	1.93	1.11	.84	.72	.64	.60
200	3.87	2.22	1.69	1.43	1.29	1.20
300	5.80	3.33	2.53	2.15	1.93	1.80
400	7.73	4.44	3.38	2.87	2.58	2.40
500	9.67	5.55	4.22	3.58	3.22	3.00
600	11.60	6.66	5.06	4.30	3.87	3.60
700	13.53	7.77	5.91	5.02	4.51	4.20
800	15.47	8.88	6.75	5.73	5.15	4.80
900	17.40	9.99	7.59	6.45	5.80	5.40
1000	19.33	11.10	8.44	7.16	6.44	6.00
2000	38.67	22.20	16.88	14.33	12.89	11.99
3000	58.00	33.31	25.32	21.49	19.33	17.99
4000	77.33	44.41	33.75	28.66	25.77	23.98
5000	96.66	55.51	42.19	35.82	32.22	29.98
6000	116.00	66.61	50.63	42.99	38.66	35.97
7000	135.33	77.71	59.07	50.15	45.10	41.97
8000	154.66	88.82	67.51	57.31	51.54	47.96
9000	174.00	99.92	75.95	64.48	57.99	53.96
10000	193.33	111.02	84.39	71.64	64.43	59.96
11000	212.66	122.12	92.82	78.81	70.87	65.95
12000	232.00	133.23	101.26	85.97	77.32	71.95
13000	251.33	144.33	109.70	93.14	83.76	77.94
14000	270.66	155.43	118.14	100.30	90.20	83.94
15000	289.99	166.53	126.58	107.46	96.65	89.93
16000	309.33	177.63	135.02	114.63	103.09	95.93
17000	328.66	188.74	143.46	121.79	109.53	101.92
18000	347.99	199.84	151.89	128.96	115.97	107.92
19000	367.33	210.94	160.33	136.12	122.42	113.91
20000	386.66	222.04	168.77	143.29	128.86	119.91
25000	483.32	277.55	210.97	179.11	161.08	149.89
30000	579.99	333.06	253.16	214.93	193.29	179.87
35000	676.65	388.57	295.35	250.75	225.51	209.84
40000	773.32	444.08	337.54	286.57	257.72	239.82
45000	869.98	499.59	379.74	322.39	289.94	269.80
50000	966.65	555.11	421.93	358.22	322.15	299.78

6½%

TERM AMOUNT	5 YEARS	10 YEARS	15 YEARS	20 YEARS	25 YEARS	30 YEARS
$ 100	1.96	1.14	.87	.75	.68	.63
200	3.91	2.27	1.74	1.49	1.35	1.26
300	5.87	3.41	2.61	2.24	2.03	1.90
400	7.83	4.54	3.48	2.98	2.70	2.53
500	9.78	5.68	4.36	3.73	3.38	3.16
600	11.74	6.81	5.23	4.47	4.05	3.79
700	13.70	7.95	6.10	5.22	4.73	4.42
800	15.65	9.08	6.97	5.96	5.40	5.06
900	17.61	10.22	7.84	6.71	6.08	5.69
1000	19.57	11.35	8.71	7.46	6.75	6.32
2000	39.13	22.71	17.42	14.91	13.50	12.64
3000	58.70	34.06	26.13	22.37	20.26	18.96
4000	78.26	45.42	34.84	29.82	27.01	25.28
5000	97.83	56.77	43.56	37.28	33.76	31.60
6000	117.40	68.13	52.27	44.73	40.51	37.92
7000	136.96	79.48	60.98	52.19	47.26	44.24
8000	156.53	90.84	69.69	59.65	54.02	50.57
9000	176.10	102.19	78.40	67.10	60.77	56.89
10000	195.66	113.55	87.11	74.56	67.52	63.21
11000	215.23	124.90	95.82	82.01	74.27	69.53
12000	234.79	136.26	104.53	89.67	81.02	75.85
13000	254.36	147.61	113.24	96.92	87.78	82.17
14000	273.93	158.97	121.95	104.38	94.53	88.49
15000	293.49	170.32	130.67	111.84	101.28	94.81
16000	313.06	181.68	139.38	119.29	108.03	101.13
17000	332.63	193.03	148.09	126.75	114.78	107.45
18000	352.19	204.39	156.80	134.20	121.54	113.77
19000	371.76	215.14	165.51	141.66	128.29	120.09
20000	391.32	227.10	174.22	149.11	135.04	126.41
25000	489.16	283.87	217.78	186.39	168.80	158.02
30000	586.99	340.64	261.33	223.67	202.56	189.62
35000	684.82	397.42	304.89	260.95	236.32	221.22
40000	782.65	454.19	348.44	298.23	270.08	252.83
45000	880.48	510.97	392.00	335.51	303.84	284.43
50000	978.31	567.74	435.55	372.79	337.60	316.03

6¾%

TERM AMOUNT	5 YEARS	10 YEARS	15 YEARS	20 YEARS	25 YEARS	30 YEARS
$ 100	1.97	1.15	.88	.76	.69	.65
200	3.94	2.30	1.77	1.52	1.38	1.30
300	5.91	3.44	2.65	2.28	2.07	1.95
400	7.87	4.59	3.54	3.04	2.76	2.59
500	9.84	5.74	4.42	3.80	3.45	3.24
600	11.81	6.89	5.31	4.56	4.15	3.89
700	13.78	8.04	6.19	5.32	4.84	4.54
800	15.75	9.19	7.08	6.08	5.53	5.19
900	17.72	10.33	7.96	6.84	6.22	5.84
1000	19.68	11.48	8.85	7.60	6.91	6.49
2000	39.37	22.96	17.70	15.21	13.82	12.97
3000	59.05	34.45	26.55	22.81	20.73	19.46
4000	78.73	45.93	35.40	30.41	27.64	25.94
5000	98.42	57.41	44.25	38.02	34.55	32.43
6000	118.10	68.89	53.09	45.62	41.45	38.92
7000	137.79	80.38	61.94	53.23	48.36	45.40
8000	157.47	91.86	70.79	60.83	55.27	51.89
9000	177.15	103.34	79.64	68.43	62.18	58.37
10000	196.84	114.82	88.49	76.04	69.09	64.86
11000	216.52	126.31	97.34	83.64	76.00	71.35
12000	236.20	137.79	106.19	91.24	82.91	77.83
13000	255.89	149.27	115.04	98.85	89.82	84.32
14000	275.57	160.75	123.89	106.45	96.73	90.80
15000	295.25	172.24	132.74	114.05	103.64	97.29
16000	314.94	183.72	141.59	121.66	110.55	103.78
17000	334.62	195.20	150.44	129.26	117.46	110.26
18000	354.30	206.68	159.23	136.87	124.36	116.75
19000	373.99	218.17	168.13	144.47	131.27	123.23
20000	393.67	229.65	176.98	152.07	138.18	129.72
25000	492.09	287.06	221.23	190.09	172.73	162.15
30000	590.51	344.47	265.47	228.11	207.27	194.58
35000	688.93	401.89	309.72	266.13	241.82	227.01
40000	787.34	459.30	353.97	304.15	276.37	259.44
45000	885.76	516.71	398.21	342.16	310.91	291.87
50000	984.18	574.12	442.46	380.18	345.46	324.30

7%

TERM AMOUNT	5 YEARS	10 YEARS	15 YEARS	20 YEARS	25 YEARS	30 YEARS
$ 100	1.98	1.16	.90	.78	.71	.67
200	3.96	2.32	1.80	1.55	1.41	1.33
300	5.94	3.48	2.70	2.33	2.12	2.00
400	7.92	4.64	3.60	3.10	2.83	2.66
500	9.90	5.81	4.49	3.88	3.53	3.33
600	11.88	6.97	5.39	4.65	4.24	3.99
700	13.86	8.13	6.29	5.43	4.95	4.66
800	15.84	9.29	7.19	6.20	5.65	5.32
900	17.82	10.45	8.09	6.98	6.36	5.99
1000	19.80	11.61	8.99	7.75	7.07	6.65
2000	39.60	23.22	17.98	15.51	14.14	13.31
3000	59.40	34.83	26.96	23.26	21.20	19.96
4000	79.21	46.44	35.95	31.01	28.27	26.61
5000	99.01	58.05	44.94	38.76	35.34	33.27
6000	116.81	69.67	53.93	46.52	42.41	39.92
7000	138.61	81.28	62.92	54.27	49.47	46.57
8000	158.41	92.89	71.91	62.02	56.54	53.22
9000	178.21	104.50	80.89	69.78	63.61	59.88
10000	198.01	116.11	89.88	77.53	70.68	66.53
11000	217.81	127.72	98.87	85.28	77.75	73.18
12000	237.62	139.33	107.86	93.04	84.81	79.84
13000	257.42	150.94	116.85	100.79	91.88	86.49
14000	277.22	162.55	125.84	108.54	98.95	93.14
15000	297.02	174.16	134.82	116.29	106.02	99.80
16000	316.82	185.77	143.81	124.05	113.08	106.45
17000	336.62	197.38	152.80	131.80	120.15	113.10
18000	356.42	209.00	161.79	139.55	127.22	119.75
19000	376.22	220.61	170.78	147.31	134.29	126.41
20000	396.03	232.22	179.77	155.06	141.36	133.06
25000	495.03	290.27	224.71	193.82	176.69	166.33
30000	594.04	348.33	269.65	232.59	212.03	199.59
35000	639.05	406.38	314.59	271.35	247.37	232.86
40000	792.05	464.44	359.53	310.12	282.71	266.12
45000	891.06	522.49	404.47	348.88	318.05	299.39
50000	990.06	580.54	449.41	387.65	353.39	332.65

7¼%

TERM AMOUNT	5 YEARS	10 YEARS	15 YEARS	20 YEARS	25 YEARS	30 YEARS
$ 100	1.99	1.17	.91	.79	.72	.68
200	3.98	2.35	1.83	1.58	1.45	1.36
300	5.98	3.52	2.74	2.37	2.17	2.05
400	7.97	4.70	3.65	3.16	2.89	2.73
500	9.96	5.87	4.56	3.95	3.61	3.41
600	11.95	7.04	5.48	4.74	4.34	4.09
700	13.94	8.22	6.39	5.53	5.06	4.78
800	15.94	9.39	7.30	6.32	5.78	5.46
900	17.93	10.57	8.22	7.11	6.51	6.14
1000	19.92	11.74	9.13	7.90	7.23	6.82
2000	39.84	23.48	18.26	15.81	14.46	13.64
3000	59.76	35.22	27.39	23.71	21.68	20.47
4000	79.68	46.96	36.51	31.61	28.91	27.29
5000	99.60	58.70	45.64	39.52	36.14	34.11
6000	119.52	70.44	54.77	47.42	43.37	40.93
7000	139.44	82.18	63.90	55.33	50.60	47.75
8000	159.36	93.92	73.03	63.23	57.82	54.57
9000	179.27	105.66	82.16	71.13	65.05	61.40
10000	199.19	117.40	91.29	79.04	72.28	68.22
11000	219.11	129.14	100.41	86.94	79.51	75.04
12000	239.03	140.88	109.54	94.84	86.74	81.86
13000	258.95	152.62	118.67	102.75	93.96	88.68
14000	278.87	164.36	127.80	110.65	101.19	95.50
15000	298.79	176.10	136.93	118.56	108.42	102.33
16000	318.71	187.84	146.06	126.46	115.65	109.15
17000	338.63	199.58	155.19	134.36	122.88	115.97
18000	358.55	211.32	164.31	142.27	130.10	122.79
19000	378.47	223.06	173.44	150.17	137.33	129.61
20000	398.39	234.80	182.57	158.07	144.56	136.43
25000	497.99	293.50	228.22	197.59	180.70	170.54
30000	597.58	352.20	273.86	237.11	216.84	204.65
35000	697.18	410.90	319.50	276.63	252.98	238.76
40000	796.78	469.60	365.14	316.15	289.12	272.87
45000	896.37	528.30	410.79	355.67	325.26	306.98
50000	995.97	587.01	456.43	395.19	361.40	341.09

7½%

TERM AMOUNT	5 YEARS	10 YEARS	15 YEARS	20 YEARS	25 YEARS	30 YEARS
$ 100	2.00	1.19	.93	.81	.74	.70
200	4.01	2.37	1.85	1.61	1.48	1.40
300	6.01	3.56	2.78	2.42	2.22	2.10
400	8.02	4.75	3.71	3.22	2.96	2.80
500	10.02	5.94	4.64	4.03	3.69	3.50
600	12.02	7.12	5.56	4.83	4.43	4.20
700	14.03	8.31	6.49	5.64	5.17	4.89
800	16.03	9.50	7.42	6.44	5.91	5.59
900	18.03	10.68	8.34	7.25	6.65	6.29
1000	20.04	11.87	9.27	8.06	7.39	6.99
2000	40.08	23.74	18.54	16.11	14.78	13.98
3000	60.11	35.61	27.81	24.17	22.17	20.98
4000	80.15	47.48	37.08	32.22	29.56	27.97
5000	100.19	59.35	46.35	40.28	36.95	34.96
6000	120.23	71.22	55.62	48.34	44.34	41.95
7000	140.27	83.09	64.89	56.39	51.73	48.95
8000	160.30	94.96	74.16	64.45	59.12	55.94
9000	180.34	106.83	83.43	72.50	66.51	62.93
10000	200.38	118.70	92.70	80.56	73.90	69.92
11000	220.42	130.57	101.97	88.62	81.29	76.91
12000	240.46	142.44	111.24	96.67	88.68	83.91
13000	260.49	154.31	120.51	104.73	96.07	90.90
14000	280.53	166.18	129.78	112.78	103.46	97.89
15000	300.57	178.05	139.05	120.84	110.85	104.88
16000	320.61	189.92	148.32	128.90	118.24	111.87
17000	340.65	201.79	157.59	136.95	125.63	118.87
18000	360.68	213.66	166.86	145.01	133.02	125.86
19000	380.72	225.53	176.13	153.06	140.41	132.85
20000	400.76	237.40	185.40	161.12	147.80	139.84
25000	500.95	296.76	231.75	201.40	184.75	174.80
30000	601.14	356.11	278.10	241.68	221.70	209.76
35000	701.33	415.46	324.46	281.96	258.65	244.73
40000	801.52	474.81	370.81	322.24	295.60	279.69
45000	901.71	534.16	417.16	362.52	332.55	314.65
50000	1001.90	593.51	463.51	402.80	369.50	349.61

7¾%

TERM AMOUNT	5 YEARS	10 YEARS	15 YEARS	20 YEARS	25 YEARS	30 YEARS
$ 100	2.02	1.20	.94	.82	.76	.72
200	4.03	2.40	1.88	1.64	1.51	1.43
300	6.05	3.60	2.82	2.46	2.27	2.15
400	8.06	4.80	3.77	3.28	3.02	2.87
500	10.08	6.00	4.71	4.10	3.78	3.58
600	12.09	7.20	5.65	4.93	4.53	4.30
700	14.11	8.40	6.59	5.75	5.29	5.01
800	16.13	9.60	7.53	6.57	6.04	5.73
900	18.14	10.80	8.47	7.39	6.80	6.45
1000	20.16	12.00	9.41	8.21	7.55	7.16
2000	40.31	24.00	18.83	16.42	15.11	14.33
3000	60.47	36.00	28.24	24.63	22.66	21.49
4000	80.63	48.00	37.65	32.84	30.21	28.66
5000	100.79	60.01	47.06	41.05	37.77	35.82
6000	120.94	72.01	56.48	49.26	45.32	42.98
7000	141.10	84.01	65.89	57.47	52.87	50.15
8000	161.26	96.01	75.30	65.68	60.43	57.31
9000	181.41	108.01	84.71	73.89	67.98	64.48
10000	201.57	120.01	94.13	82.09	75.53	71.64
11000	221.73	132.01	103.54	90.30	83.09	78.81
12000	241.88	144.01	112.95	98.51	90.64	85.97
13000	262.04	156.01	122.37	106.72	98.19	93.13
14000	282.20	168.02	131.78	114.93	105.75	100.30
15000	302.36	180.02	141.19	123.14	113.30	107.46
16000	322.51	192.02	150.60	131.35	120.85	114.63
17000	342.67	204.02	160.02	139.56	128.41	121.79
18000	362.83	216.02	169.43	147.77	135.96	128.95
19000	382.98	228.02	178.84	155.98	143.51	136.12
20000	403.14	240.02	188.26	164.19	151.07	143.28
25000	503.93	300.03	235.32	205.24	188.83	179.10
30000	604.71	360.03	282.38	246.28	226.60	214.92
35000	705.50	420.04	329.45	287.33	264.36	250.74
40000	806.28	480.04	376.51	328.38	302.13	286.56
45000	907.07	540.05	423.57	369.43	339.90	322.38
50000	1007.85	600.05	470.64	410.47	377.66	358.21

8%

TERM AMOUNT	5 YEARS	10 YEARS	15 YEARS	20 YEARS	25 YEARS	30 YEARS
$ 100	2.03	1.21	.96	.84	.77	.73
200	4.06	2.43	1.91	1.67	1.54	1.47
300	6.08	3.64	2.87	2.51	2.32	2.20
400	8.11	4.85	3.82	3.35	3.09	2.94
500	10.14	6.07	4.78	4.18	3.86	3.67
600	12.17	7.28	5.73	5.02	4.63	4.40
700	14.19	8.49	6.69	5.86	5.40	5.14
800	16.22	9.71	7.65	6.69	6.17	5.87
900	18.25	10.92	8.60	7.53	6.95	6.60
1000	20.28	12.13	9.56	8.36	7.72	7.34
2000	40.55	24.27	19.11	16.73	15.44	14.68
3000	60.83	36.40	28.67	25.09	23.15	22.01
4000	81.11	48.53	38.23	33.46	30.87	29.35
5000	101.38	60.66	47.78	41.82	38.59	36.69
6000	121.66	72.80	57.34	50.19	46.31	44.03
7000	141.94	84.93	66.90	58.55	54.03	51.36
8000	162.21	97.06	76.45	66.91	61.74	58.70
9000	182.49	109.19	86.01	75.28	69.46	66.04
10000	202.76	121.33	95.56	83.64	77.18	73.38
11000	223.04	133.46	105.12	92.01	84.90	80.71
12000	243.32	145.59	114.68	100.37	92.62	88.05
13000	263.59	157.73	124.23	108.74	100.34	95.39
14000	283.87	169.86	133.79	117.10	108.05	102.73
15000	304.15	181.99	143.35	125.47	115.77	110.06
16000	324.42	194.12	152.90	133.83	123.49	117.40
17000	344.70	206.26	162.46	142.19	131.21	124.74
18000	364.98	218.39	172.02	150.56	138.93	132.08
19000	385.25	230.52	181.57	158.92	146.64	139.41
20000	405.53	242.66	191.13	167.29	154.36	146.75
25000	506.91	303.32	238.91	209.11	192.95	183.44
30000	608.29	363.98	286.69	250.93	231.54	220.13
35000	709.68	424.65	334.48	292.75	270.13	256.82
40000	811.06	485.31	382.26	334.57	308.72	293.50
45000	912.44	545.97	430.04	376.40	347.32	330.19
50000	1013.82	606.64	477.82	418.22	385.91	366.88

INDEX